Printed by Lakeside Press
PO Box 1075
Willmar, MN 56201 USA
(320) 235-5849

Thank you to Joanne Glor, Debbie Holmquist,
Rebecca Spartz, Chris Voth, Mark Peterson and
especially my wife Julie,
for their support and assistance.

———————

greed

BY: GLENN JOPLIN

Contents

Greed

Dr. Sorenson was feeling very proud of himself. He was beginning to come out of the stupor he had been in since he was first drugged. He could hardly stand up or talk. He had been able to cheek the last two pills they gave him and spit them out in his hand. Now, if he could only get rid of this big ape who insisted on being with him all the time, even when he went to the bathroom. What was he doing to the bed sheet? Why was he cutting it up?

Greed
Chapter One

Ken checked the calendar on his iPhone. Death Review at 8:00 a.m. was at the top of the list for Monday morning. Ken's supervisor, Jane Carlson, insisted that all of her staff have iPhones so she could inform them of important meetings and significant events related to work at the hospital.

Death reviews are held as soon as possible after the death of a patient, no matter what the cause of death is. The objective of the review is to go over in detail all the information available regarding the patient who died. It was the hospital and state policy to conduct such reviews with the idea that mistakes or errors might be identified and eliminated. Most of the time the reviews did not find any mistakes but sometimes they did result in improved hospital procedures.

The hospital also holds incident reviews, where serious incidents occur, but do not include the death of a patient. Examples are assaults on patients or staff, misuse of or overdose on medication, and illicit use of drugs. Ann Peterson, Director of Nursing, is the staff person who is responsible for arranging the incident reviews, but any supervisor can request that one be held.

Death reviews are automatic and are called at the earliest possible time. Participation is mandatory. Requests to be excused from a death review have to be approved by the Medical Director.

Permanent members on the death review team at Arrowhead Hospital include the Medical Director, Director of Nursing, Social Services Director, and the Hospital Administrator. Additional members include staff who were directly associated with the patient's care, especially staff who were on duty when the patient died.

Ken Wold is the social worker assigned to the hospital unit where the patient died. He has been employed at the hospital for fifteen years and is expected to be the next Social Services Director when Mrs. Carlson retires. Ken is seen by other staff as being very efficient, easy to get along with, and very competent in his job. He would be a good leader.

His personal life was not as good. He and his wife Diane were divorced after he found out she was having an affair with another teacher.

Ken and Diane met at college, went together for two years, and were married soon after they graduated. They found jobs in the same town and agreed to wait for a few years to have children. The children arrived a little sooner than they planned, and changed their lives completely, but they quickly adjusted.

Tom was ten years old and Jack was eight when their parents divorced, and it was a difficult time for everyone. Diane and Ken agreed to share custody and they tried to make the situation work out as well as possible. They agreed not to involve their children in their conflicts and not to speak badly about the other parent in front of the boys.

Ken was an athlete in high school and usually played sports with the boys when it was his weekend to have them. Diane and Ken agreed that the boys would live with Diane, but Ken would get them every other weekend. Diane encouraged the boy's involvement in sports and would often attend their games. Ken was usually one of the coaches on the baseball and basketball teams.

Chapter Two

While sitting at the conference table waiting for the rest of the team to arrive, Ken reflected on the weekend he had shared with Becky. "Now this relationship has some promise." He said to himself. Ken first became aware of Becky's existence when he was working out at the local YMCA. He could not keep his eyes off her. She not only had a great body, she was also the most beautiful woman he had ever seen. Ken usually worked on the weights and Becky used the aerobic machines. Ken became more interested in aerobics and changed his workout schedule to the same days and hours as Becky. He was slowly getting up enough nerve to talk to her. One evening, Ken brought Tom into the emergency room after he twisted an ankle in a basketball game. Becky was the admitting nurse. Ken could not believe his good luck. It took Ken several months and a few more trips to the emergency room to get up the nerve to ask Becky to go out with him. She was six years younger than he was and he was sure she would have several other men interested in dating her. Becky was attracted to Ken and did some research on her own after their first meeting. She discovered that he was a very respected social worker at the hospital and a leader in the community. He was on the school board and was seen as a loving father to his sons. She was also impressed with the boys and the way they interacted with their father. She was beginning to wonder if he was ever going to ask her out.

Ken was a little old for Becky, but he seemed like the kind of person she would like to know better. She accepted his invitation for coffee and they had been dating ever since.

Ken's sons would have preferred that their parents get back together, but that possibility no longer existed after their mother married another teacher. Tom and Jack adored Becky and, next to their mother, Becky would be the woman they would pick for their father.

The relationship between Ken and Becky was starting to get serious and they were even talking about taking a vacation together. Ken had finally gotten over the divorce and he was feeling better than he had for several years. The future was looking good.

Chapter Three

Dr. Rogers, the unit psychiatrist, walked into the conference room. "Lets get this over with. I have a lot of patients to see." "What a pompous ass," Ken thought to himself. Dr. Joseph Rogers had been employed at the hospital for eight years. During that time he had managed to get almost everyone angry with him for something he did or said. The psychiatrist on the unit needs to approve all the major decisions regarding patients and many of Dr. Rogers' decisions did not make sense.

Dr. Rogers would not listen to other staff or take their advice. Many of the social workers in the community tried to get patients transferred to other doctors because of Dr. Rogers' unwillingness to work with them in treatment and discharge planning. Unit staff and community workers would put together a discharge plan for a patient and Dr. Rogers would shoot the plan down for some reason that did not make sense. It often seemed like he would torpedo a discharge plan just because he had the power to do so. He seemed to enjoy the conflict.

Several years ago Ken decided he would try to avoid conflicts with Dr. Rogers by asking his opinion first, before developing a treatment or discharge plan. Even that did not work.

Dr. Rogers would even disagree with his own plan. When this was brought to his attention, he would get upset and give some obscure reason for his decision.

Dr. Rogers seemed to have a very narrow band of medications he favored and he seldom strayed from them, even when new medications came out. He would get upset when he was informed that a doctor in the community changed a patient's medications as soon as he was discharged.

Dr. Rogers was from the east coast and attended private and Ivy League schools. He never failed to get his background into the conversation and seemed to put down others, even other psychiatrists, for not having the same educational advantages.

Many of the staff on a psychiatric unit have worked on the unit for twenty or thirty years. Their experience is often invaluable to making the unit work smoothly and minimize the problems that often occur in working with mentally ill patients. They have a wide variety of responsibilities and one of those responsibilities is to distribute medications to patients. Staff have seen the effect medications have on people, how the patient responds, and the side effects which accompany most medications. During patient conferences, Dr. Rogers would become upset if a staff member mentioned anything about medication. It got to the point that staff would not express any opinions about patient care when Dr. Rogers was in the room. He would dominate the conversation and would put down the comments made by others. It was not unusual for staff to request a transfer to another unit in order to avoid working with Dr. Rogers.

The hospital administrator and the medical director had talked to Dr. Rogers several times about his attitude and the impact he was having on hospital staff and people in the community. They tried to get him to be a positive leader. He would change his behavior for a short time, but it would not last long. County officials would often complain about Dr. Rogers to the hospital administrator and would threaten to send their patients to other hospitals. Some judges refused to allow Dr. Rogers to testify at commitment hearings because of his attitude and arrogance.

Although the hospital administrator and medical director wanted to fire Dr. Rogers, and they had plenty of reasons to do so, their hands were tied. It was better to have a psychiatrist, even one with Dr. Roger's shortcomings, than none at all. The hospital needed Dr. Rogers. It was extremely hard to find and hire psychiatrists. Sometimes it would take a year or more to find a replacement. Retired psychiatrists would agree to work for a few months, but they were also hard to find.

Chapter Four

Ann Peterson, the Nursing Director, Chaired the Death Review. She was just the opposite of Dr. Rogers. Everyone liked her. She was willing to listen to other staff and staff knew that even though they might not agree with her decision, it was carefully thought out. Staff members often said that Ann ran the hospital. She seemed to be involved in every major decision. Ann had been working at the hospital for twenty-four years and had worked her way up the ladder of responsibility. The older staff could remember how well she handled herself when she first became employed at the hospital. Most new employees are anxious and sometimes afraid when they start work in a mental health unit. It takes time to get used to mentally ill patients and the different symptoms they exhibit. Beginning with the first day, Ann demonstrated a special talent in working with mental patients. She seemed to know instinctively what was the right thing to say or do when relating to patients and their behavior.

"Let's get started," Ann said. "Thomas Howell was found dead in his room around 10 p.m. on Friday, August 16. It appears that he hanged himself by tying strips cut from a bed sheet to a metal guard over the light fixture and stepping off a chair. We do not have a lot of information on Mr. Howell because he just arrived on Thursday, August 15, with a minimum of paper work. Unit staff had just started their admission evaluations on Friday."

"According to the very limited amount of information in his chart, Mr. Howell was very unsteady and dazed, making nonsensical statements when he arrived. Law Enforcement was called immediately after he was found and they are still conducting their investigation. As of now, law enforcement and our staff see the incident as a suicide."

"I saw him around 5 p.m. Thursday and I did not notice any major problems," said Dr. Rogers. "He appeared to be very tired and sleepy, but I thought his medication was appropriate." "Must have been on one of Doc's favorite meds." Ken thought to himself.

"Who found him?" asked Dr. Williams, the Medical Director. "Chad Turnquist," said Ann Peterson. "Who is he?" asked Ken, "I have never heard of him." "He is a temporary nursing assistant who just started work a few days ago," responded Ann. "Why isn't he at the death review?" asked Dr. Williams.

"He quit on Saturday. He told me he was very upset with finding Mr. Howell and I agreed that this might not be the best place for him to work," said Dr. Rogers.

"You told Mr. Turnquist he could leave?" asked Mr. Tolliver, incredulously, looking at the medical director as if he was saying, "Why did we ever hire this person."

"Yes," said Dr. Rogers. "Turnquist said he didn't care about being paid. He just wanted to get out of here. It was a very traumatic experience for him."

Mr. Tolliver was reluctant to embarrass Dr. Rogers in front of the other staff, but he told himself that this was one more thing he needed to talk with Dr. Rogers about when they meet with the medical director. We may have to let Dr. Rogers go, he said to himself. This is just too much.

"Mr. Howell was apparently referred by a psychiatrist in Wisconsin," continued Mrs. Peterson.

"I took the call and approved the transfer," said Dr. Rogers.

"Why didn't you go through the admission process?" asked Ken, who was not afraid to challenge Dr. Rogers when he thought he made a mistake.

"The referring psychiatrist, Dr. Benton, is a friend of mine from college and called me directly Thursday afternoon," said Dr. Rogers. "I thought it was too late to involve Admissions and that we could wait until Friday to do the admissions workup."

"But we accept patients around the clock," said Ken. "How is this admission any different from the others?"

"I was just trying to be helpful," responded Dr. Rogers who was beginning to feel irritated with all the questions. "Look, I have patients to see. It appears to me that this is very cut and dried. The patient hung himself. Do we have to go through all these details?"

"Yes," replied the Medical Director, Dr. Williams, who was becoming increasingly irritated with Dr. Rogers and his repeated violations of hospital policy. "I'm going to ask the police department to get more involved, just so we can have everything covered in case we get sued by someone," said Dr. Williams.

"I don't see any reason for that," said Dr. Rogers. "But, do whatever you think is necessary."

After the meeting, Ken walked back to his office with his supervisor, Jane Carlson. "Dr. Rogers never fails to amaze me with his antics," said Jane. "He violated numerous hospital procedures with the way he handled this patient."

"Yeah," replied Ken. "Mr. Tolliver and Dr. Williams appeared to be very upset with Rogers, but they will probably just slap his wrists and let him continue to screw up."

"Sooner or later his behavior will get us all in trouble."

Chapter Five

Ken had a 10:00 a.m. meeting with April to discuss her discharge and he was looking forward to it. When they first met, she was twenty years old and it was her first admission. Her diagnosis was schizophrenia and she was very difficult to work with, especially when she was not taking her medication properly. She was hearing voices telling her she was a bad person and telling her what to do. When she was hearing the voices, she thought they were real and she was constantly replying to them as if she was talking to another person. Ken remembered that her parents had a hard time accepting her illness.

Her parents thought April was on drugs and needed chemical dependency treatment. They had high expectations for April and they had a difficult time accepting the diagnosis, and the ramifications that went with it.

April Henderson had been through a lot since her first hospitalization. When she was not taking her medications she would often end up on the streets running from pimps and men who abuse women and take advantage of their weakness. She seemed to have an inner strength that got her out of many situations and she was always joking around, even about her illness. April seemed to respond well to medication, but she had a hard time staying on medication because of the side effects. She said the side effects made her feel listless and like a zombie. "Do you still hear voices?" asked Ken.

"Yeah, but they are not as bad as when I first came to the hospital," responded April.

"How about the side effects?" asked Ken.

"They are still there, but I can deal with them. They don't seem to be as bad with the medications Dr. Rogers prescribed." April said. Ken always wondered how honest patients were with him. They were so anxious to be discharged that they would say anything to get out of the hospital.

"We previously talked about you going to a halfway house and slowly working toward independence. Is that still the plan?" "Yeah," responded April. "My parents invited me to stay with them, but we always seem to get into arguments, resulting in my leaving, and they hate my smoking. Smoking is the only good thing in my life, and I can't give that up."

"We want you to continue to work with the community program," said Ken. "They can check on you regularly and help you stay on your medication."

"Yeah," said April. "I like most of the workers and they have been helpful in the past when I had problems. I always think I can do it alone and that I don't need any help or medication. That's when I get in trouble and hit the streets. The voices become so natural to me that I don't believe I need help."

"That's good insight," said Ken. "I wish there was some way you could stop and ask for help when you start down that path. Try calling me at work when you start to have problems, and I can get help for you right away. Here is my card."

"OK," said April. Ken wished there was some way he could help April more, but he knew there was only so much he or anyone else could do.

"Before you go," said Ken. "What do you know about the guy who recently died on the unit?"

"I did not get to know him," said April. "The other patients said he was really doped up. I can't see how he was able to hang himself. He could hardly stand up. Apparently, he was mumbling something, but no one could understand him. That new guy on staff, Chad, seemed to spend a lot of time with the new patient and ignored the rest of us."

Chapter Six

As he was walking to the administration building, Ken looked back on his fifteen years on the mental health unit. He had learned a lot. Dennis Werkman, the psychologist on the unit and a good friend, said a person really does not understand mental illness until they have worked in a unit like this. The locked mental health unit is the end of the line, where the most difficult patients end up. Most of the patients are committed by the court.

Ken thought about the girls who had cut marks on their arms, usually girls with a history of depression and abuse. The girls would often wear long sleeve blouses to hide the cuts.

Sometimes, after their arms were full of cuts, they would start cutting their legs. They would usually alternate their arms and cut in different places so the cuts would have time to heal. They would seldom cut deep enough to cause death, but deep enough for them to watch the blood ooze out of the cut. The deeper the cut, the better they would feel, and the harder it would be to stop the bleeding with a bandage. Sometimes it would be necessary to take them to the emergency room to stitch up the wound.

Schizophrenia was a mental illness that fascinated Ken. Each patient's symptoms seemed to be unique. One patient might hear voices telling him to do something. Another patient might see things no one else can see, such as spiders crawling up a wall. Ken remembered recently completing a report on a young man. During the interview, Ken said to himself. "This guy is not mentally ill." Then the patient said. "I have this radio in my tooth and I can hear the FBI and CIA talking to each other." The interesting thing was that these patients actually believed what they were experiencing. This was reality to them.

The bipolar diagnosis, where people experience symptoms of depression and mania at different times, is a common illness at the hospital. Some of the patients become so depressed that they try to commit suicide. The manic patients sometimes required physical interventions. Ken remembered one manic patient who was very big and muscular. He was tearing the unit apart, throwing furniture, yelling and screaming. It took six staff members to hold him down long enough to give him a shot to calm him down. One staff member broke his wrist while he was trying to take the patient down. In the manic stage, people may stay awake for days at a time and seem to be able to accomplish many things in a short period of time.

After working with patients for several years Ken came to realize that one of the most difficult things for them to do is to stay on their medication, even though they know it helps them and keeps them out of trouble. Patients told him how terrible the medications made them feel. Some of them would walk in a shuffle and act like zombies, as April said. Ken understood when patients told him about the difficult decisions they had to make about medications. Stay on the medications and put up with the side effects, or drop the medications and return to experiencing the symptoms of their illness.

Some of the patients developed tardive dyskinesia, a chronic disorder of the nervous system characterized by involuntary jerky movements. With some patients, their tongues would go in and out of their mouths involuntarily. Other patients would smack their lips and make facial grimaces. Still others would fling their hands in the air and their heads would go back and forth. Patients who experienced tardive dyskinesia would have to take additional medication to control these symptoms.

Ken often thought that it should be a prerequisite for staff, especially psychiatrists who prescribe the medications, to take the medication to see what patients have to go through. It was not hard to talk himself out of volunteering for such an experience.

Ken felt especially sorry for patients who are anorexic. Some patients die in spite of all the efforts to save them. They may look like skeletons and still think they are overweight. Even forced feeding did not work with some patients. Ken thought about some of the parents of patients he had worked with. The parents and loved ones also suffer greatly. Parents become very frustrated and upset when they try to find help for their child who refuses to cooperate. In order to get a court order to make a person participate in treatment, the mentally ill person must often be seen as a danger to themselves or others.

Chapter Seven

Every Wednesday, when both of them have the time, Ken and John Davis meet at the Riverside Inn for a drink after work. They were childhood friends who grew up together in a nearby suburb. They played sports together in high school and attended the same college. John received a football scholarship and played tight end on the college team. Ken did not receive a scholarship, but he was a big supporter of the team, attending all the games. Ken majored in social work and John majored in law enforcement. John's father was a policeman and both John and Ken had great respect for him. Ken's father died in a car accident when Ken was ten years old and John's father treated Ken like he was his son, involving him in many family activities. Ken and John were very close friends as adults and their families often vacationed together before Ken became divorced. John had been Ken's best man at his wedding and was there for Ken to talk to when he had marital problems. John was married, had four children, with another child on the way.

John had been a police officer for fifteen years and was promoted to detective several years ago. Ken was proud of his friend and expected John to keep climbing the professional ladder. Ken often thought John would make a good Chief of Police someday.

"We had a suicide this past weekend." Ken said.

"Yeah," said John. "I did not catch the case, but I heard about it. Some guy hung himself?"

"It was on my unit so I attended the death review Monday," said Ken. "Dr. Rogers was his usual sweet self. There is something strange about the whole situation," Ken said.

"What do you mean?" asked John.

"Well, the victim was a new patient and we had very little information on him. Dr. Rogers was involved in every phase of his hospitalization, even as far as the hiring of the new staff member who found the patient hanging."

John smiled," There is that detective mind starting to work." They both laughed, because Ken had always been interested in John's work and often volunteered suggestions when it came to the cases John was working on. "Remember that shooting a year ago?" John said. "You almost solved that case single-handedly." They both laughed.

"Yeah, but something is not right," said Ken. "I can feel it in my bones."

"But the case has been cleared," said John. "The guy hung himself, according to Detective Morris."

"Yeah, I know, I suppose I had better drop it." They went on to talk about the local high school football teams.

Chapter Eight

Ken could not get the suicide out of his mind as he sat at his desk on the mental health unit. The whole thing did not make sense. There were too many unanswered questions. But, to his knowledge, no one else seemed to be concerned. Everyone appeared to accept the incident as just another suicide. The police had closed the case, the death review was completed with no recommendations, and all the proper documents had been signed. "I am going to check it out anyway." Ken said to himself. "I am not going to be satisfied until I have more answers to my questions."

The first thing Ken decided to do was to get more information on the patient who supposedly had committed suicide. He began to look for the patient's chart, only to find that it was checked out to Dr. Rogers, and, according to the records, had been checked out to him since the patient died. Ken approached Dr. Rogers and asked him if he still had the chart. Dr. Rogers said. "What do you want with the chart?"

"I just want to read the chart to see if there is anything I need to do." said Ken. "I usually see every patient and write a report on them, but I did not have time to see this patient before he committed suicide."

"Well, you don't have to write a report on Howell because he is dead," said Dr. Rogers.

"Are you going to give me the chart or am I going to have to go to Dr. Williams to get it?" Ken asked.

"Oh what the hell, take the damn thing," responded Dr. Rogers. "There is nothing in there anyway. You are not the only one that did not have time to write a report. I left shortly after he arrived. I just had time to write a few notes and review his medication."

"Thanks," said Ken.

Ken took the chart back to his office to read when he had time. He had a discharge meeting with a patient, the patient's family, and the county social worker. Two new patients had arrived, and he had to see them, call their county social workers, and complete their intake reports. The county workers were usually involved in getting patients admitted to the hospital and often knew the patients better than anyone. Sometimes the social worker would bring the patient to the hospital, but often they would call the police and ask them to transport the patient, especially the unruly ones. New patients were usually off their medications and deep into the reality of their illness. The county social workers usually had no influence on which unit the patient was assigned to, but they often tried to keep the patient from going to the unit on which Dr. Rogers worked.

Ken finally found some time to go over Mr. Howell's chart. As he read the limited chart, he seemed to have more questions than answers. There were some brief admission notes by the nurses on duty, but most of the information was hand written by Dr. Rogers and it was very vague. Who was Thomas Howell and who was the staff member Chad Turnquist? What stood out was the lack of information on both of the men. It was interesting that there were no notes in the chart written by Turnquist, the staff member who is supposed to have spent the most time with Howell.

Ken knew he could not drop his search for answers in the suicide until he had more information that made sense. He simply had to get more information on the dead patient, if nothing else than to satisfy his own curiosity.

Ken knew, from previous experience, that it would be difficult and very time consuming to search for more information on Mr. Howell. When he had tried to get information on previous patients, Ken had repeatedly run into the issue of confidentiality. It seemed to be like a golden rule. Patient information is sacred and is not to be shared with anyone unless appropriate permission is granted. Ken could understand the need for privacy. He certainly would not want his personal information shared with others without his permission. He remembered all the things he and his ex-wife talked about in marriage counseling. Even though this would make his work much harder, Ken told himself that he owed it to the patient to find out the truth.

Ken decided to ask his supervisor, Jane Carlson, if he could use hospital time to follow up on some of the questions he had. Jane liked and respected Ken and she knew he would not abuse it if she approved the request. She gave him limited approval, telling him it could not interfere with his normal work load.

Chapter Nine

At their weekly meeting, Ken told John about his intentions to get more information about the dead patient and about Dr. Roger's reluctance to give him the chart on the new patient. John offered to help Ken if he needed help.

Dr. Benton, the referring psychiatrist from Wisconsin, would be a good place to start, Ken decided. Ken needed to check out all of the limited information in the chart and find out if there was anything to support his suspicions. There was no address or telephone number for Dr. Benton in the chart. Ken found this to be strange, and quickly realized that it may take longer and be more difficult than he originally expected. Ken was reluctant to ask Dr. Rogers for more information on Dr. Benton so Ken proceeded to try to track him down the hard way.

Ken began with the Provider Directory for professionals in the state of Wisconsin. This was a list of all medical providers approved by one of the Medicare insurance plans. Ken checked the website for the insurance plan in Wisconsin and found five doctors with the name of Benton. Two of the doctors were psychiatrists. One was Dr. Anita Benton who was a professor of medicine at the University of Wisconsin in Madison. The other psychiatrist was Dr. Alex Benton who was employed at Albany Pharmaceuticals in Milwaukee.

It was Ken's experience that most medical professionals continue to practice their professions on a part time basis even though they work in a university or other setting. They continue their practice for several reasons. Such as: to make more money, to keep up with the changes in their profession, and as something they can fall back on if they leave their present position.

After playing telephone tag for a week, Ken finally reached Dr. Anita Benton. He asked her if she had referred a patient to the hospital in Lawrence. She said she had never referred a patient to any hospital in Minnesota. Dr. Alex Benton was even more difficult to contact.

During the process of trying to contact Dr. Alex Benton, Ken discovered that he was a high level administrator at a pharmaceutical company. Ken wondered how a high level administrator could be involved in referring a patient to his hospital.

Chapter Ten

Dr. Alex Benton was very much aware of Ken's efforts to contact him and was trying to avoid talking to him, hoping that Ken would give up. Dr. Rogers and Dr. Benton talked often over the telephone and Dr. Rogers told Dr. Benton that Ken was asking questions about the suicide. Dr. Benton was upset with Dr. Rogers for using his name and was trying to figure out a way to deal with Ken.

Dr. Benton was vice president at Albany Pharmaceuticals and one of his administrative assignments, other than Director of Research, was Security. Dr. Benton met Dr. Rogers in college, and they attended the same medical school. They had worked together in different mental health settings before getting their present jobs. Both men were heavily invested in Albany Pharmaceutical and their investments had paid off richly the past few years as new psychiatric medications were developed by the company. Dr. Benton had developed the reputation as a brilliant leader in the company. Several new successful medications had been developed by the research division, and the huge growth of the company was partly attributed to Dr. Benton's leadership.

Even though Dr. Benton had graduated from a prestigious college, he had never been seen as one of the elite because he was not born into the same culture as Dr. Rogers. Alex Benton was born and raised in the South. His father was a farmer and had a fourth grade education. His mother had a ninth grade education. Alex was an only child and his parents stressed the need for him to make something of himself. He saw poverty all around and was determined from an early age to be successful and rich. He quickly saw education as a way out and excelled in the classroom. Because of his excellent grades, and high scores on college admission tests, Alex was able to get scholarship offers to the best schools in the South. But, Alex wanted more. He wanted to go to an Ivy League College. He achieved his goal and received full scholarships to college and medical school.

Alex had a difficult time adapting to the culture on the East Coast and he felt like he was not accepted by the other students. Joe Rogers felt sorry for him and invited him to his home during school breaks. Alex felt accepted by Joe's family and ended up marrying a cousin of Joe.

Ken had tried to contact Dr. Benton so many times that he became friendly with Amy Wheeler, one of the receptionists at Albany Pharmaceuticals. During one call, Ken happened to mention the name of Thomas Howell to Amy. Amy said the name was familiar, but she could not remember where she heard the name or in what context she had heard it.

Two weeks after unsuccessfully trying to contact Dr. Benton, Dr. Rogers walked into Ken's office and handed him an envelope. Dr. Rogers was unusually pleasant and appeared to be nervous. "If you still have that patient's chart, here is more information on him," said Dr. Rogers. "Would you make sure it gets in the chart?"

"Thanks," said Ken. "By the way, do you know how I can reach Dr. Benton, the psychiatrist who referred Mr. Howell? I tried to reach him several times and did not get a response."

"He seems to be very busy," responded Dr. Rogers. "I have a hard time getting hold of him too. We went to college and medical school together and he is married to my cousin. We get together sometimes and often meet at psychiatric conferences," said Dr. Rogers.

"Is Dr. Benton employed at Albany Pharmaceuticals?" asked Ken.

"Yes," responded Dr. Rogers. "He has worked there for a long time. He is on the management team."

"Does he still see patients?" asked Ken. "I think he sees patients at Albany Hospital," responded Dr. Rogers. "Most psychiatrists in management continue to see patients on a part time basis to stay sharp."

"Would you make sure that information gets in the chart?" asked Dr. Rogers. "Sure," said Ken. "I will take care of it."

Ken opened the envelope and found a typical summary of a patient's hospitalization.

Albany Hospital   August 19, 2012
Mental Health Unit
Thomas Howell # 26459

Mr. Howell was admitted to the ER unit at 11 p.m. on Tuesday, August 14, 2012. He was brought to the hospital by law enforcement after he was found wandering in the street.

He appeared to be dazed, talking about aliens trying to kill him. He said the aliens had poisoned his food. Mr. Howell was transferred to the psychiatric unit and started on medication. There is no information currently available on Mr. Howell's background. This is his first hospitalization at Albany Hospital. Social Service staff will try to find more information on him. Because of limited bed space in the psychiatric unit, Mr. Howell will be transferred to another facility that has space to accommodate him. Additional information received after he is discharged will be sent to the new facility. Diagnosis: Schizophrenia

Dr. Alex Benton M.D. Psychiatrist

After reading the letter, Ken was even more suspicious. The report was very short and resulted in even more questions. Things just don't add up, he said to himself.

Ken was glad to have John Davis to talk to. If he told other people what he was doing and thinking, they would probably laugh at him.

At their weekly meeting at the Riverside Inn, Ken filled John in on his progress. "I think Dr. Benton tried to appease me by sending a short summary of Thomas Howell's hospitalization in Wisconsin." Ken told John. "It just increased my curiosity."

"Are you writing all this down?" asked John. "Oh yes. You taught me to record everything. Remember?" They both laughed. "I started a journal which I keep in my office and write in it almost every day." Said Ken. "You said it is always very important to write everything down in case you miss something and have to go back and review your work. I even keep track of the times I beat you in basketball."

"That list can't be very long," responded John. John thought to himself that Ken enjoyed this detective work. He would have been a good officer. He seemed to have the right temperament for it.

Ken continued. "There are just so many unanswered questions. Who is this Thomas Howell? Most people of his age with similar symptoms have a long history of mental illness and their chart is an inch thick. They usually have several previous hospitalizations."

"They pop up in the mental health system every so often, for one reason or another, and are well known by the time they get to be his age. Why was he transferred to Arrowhead Hospital, out of state and hundreds of miles from Milwaukee? What is the relationship between Dr. Rogers and Dr. Benton? Who is this Chad Turnquist and where is he? How can an employee be hired and start his employment so quickly, without background checks, and quit so fast with no follow up information? The more I think about it, the more questions I have"

Chapter Eleven

Dr. Benton was surprised when security was added to his company responsibilities three years ago. He knew security was important but he could not see how it was related to his experience and training. Research and developing new medications was his primary interest. It did not take Dr. Benton long to figure out that security was very important and would be a good thing for him to have on his resume. Included in security was patent protection, making sure other companies did not discover what research his company was working on, and essentially making sure Albany Pharmaceuticals was making money.

Making money for the company also meant Dr. Benton was making money for himself because he had all of his money invested in the company.

Ever since Dr. Benton assumed responsibility for security, he had slowly put together a security staff that was entirely responsible to him and that reported to him directly. He knew everything about the company and the leaders, his bosses. His knowledge made him even more influential in the company and helped him to get even closer to his goal of becoming CEO. Dr. Benton even surprised himself as to how far he would go to gain control. Several staff had experienced his wrath and were either demoted or no longer with the company. In just a few years Dr. Benton had become a feared man that no one wanted to cross. His reputation could not help but to influence the way he felt about himself. He saw himself as being able to do anything he wanted to do, and as being in complete control.

Not being able to control Ken Wold and his continual prying was becoming a big problem for him.

Chapter Twelve

Dr. Benton assumed that sending the intake summary on Howell worked and that Ken was satisfied and was no longer interested in making trouble. Dr. Benton was wrong. Ken went to the personnel office to get more information on Chad Turnquist, the mysterious staff member who suddenly appeared and disappeared. The personnel secretary referred Ken to the Personnel Director, George Spangler. George told Ken that he could not give him any information on employees because it was privileged information. Ken expected this response because George was very strict about the rules regarding personnel. They were friends, and fishing buddies, but George would not budge when it came to stretching the rules. Ken was mildly upset by George's attitude, but he told himself that he would be glad to have George on his side if someone was looking for information on him. Most people have things in their history that they really don't want the public to know about.

Ken also knew that his angry feelings were not directed at George. He was becoming increasingly agitated about his inability to get information. Maybe I should just give up and quit this search, Ken said to himself.

Ken considered the option of working his way up the ladder of responsibility. He asked George if he could get the information on Turnquist if the hospital administrator approved the request. George replied that he would release the file if ordered to do so, but he would advise Mr. Tolliver, the hospital administrator, not to release the information. He said a court order was the right way to have the file released.

There was one possibility left to find information about Chad Turnquist. Ken decided to talk with all staff that may have encountered Turnquist during his brief employment. What Ken found out was that Turnquist was a very private person who was not sociable and who divulged very little information. He avoided coffee sessions and associated with the patients when other staff took a break for coffee. The few things staff did pick up were that Turnquist had previously worked in Wisconsin and that he somehow knew Dr. Rogers.

He and Dr. Rogers had been seen talking together on several occasions, but never in the presence of other staff.

Ken reviewed the limited information he had gleaned over the past few weeks. Dr. Rogers was acquainted with Dr. Benton who referred Thomas Howell. Dr. Rogers also had some type of relationship with Chad Turnquist who spent a lot of time with Howell after he was admitted. Dr. Benton, Thomas Howell, and Chad Turnquist were all from Wisconsin.

"That's not much." Ken said to himself.

Chapter Thirteen

At their weekly meeting at the Riverside Inn, Ken and John talked about their children and the sports teams they were on. Sometimes the boys were on the same team and sometime they were on opposing teams. Both Ken and John were assistant coaches on the teams.

John asked Ken about his love life, specifically about Becky.

"When are we going to meet her?" asked John. "Sarah wants to invite you over to our house for dinner and she wants to meet Becky and give her approval. You know how much Sarah likes you. She doesn't want to see you get hurt again."

"It's still going well," responded Ken. "We are even talking about taking a short vacation together. That will be a good test. She has already passed one major test, my boys. They think she is great and that is important to me. I'm still worried about our age difference and how that will have an impact on our relationship in the long run. So far it has not been an issue. Tell Sarah to give me a few more weeks and then I will take her up on that offer."

Ken filled John in on his limited detective work regarding Chad Turnquist. "You couldn't get me a court order to look at his file, could you?" asked Ken.

"It's doubtful. The death was declared a suicide by the coroner, and our investigation could not find anything that was suspicious," replied John. "Maybe it was just a suicide.

What I can do is put Turnquist's name in our data base to see if he has a prior criminal history. Why are you checking him out?" asked John.

"Nothing about the suicide makes sense," replied Ken. "If I could get some answers to my questions, I might feel better and drop the whole thing. I seem to be the only person that thinks something is wrong. An out of state stranger is admitted to the hospital under unusual circumstances, and commits suicide a day later. A new staff member is closely involved in the incident and disappears before anyone can talk with him. Dr. Rogers is involved in the hiring and the disappearance of the staff member. I just can't get it out of my mind. There is one more thing. The referring psychiatrist, Dr. Benton, Thomas Howell, the patient, and Chad Turnquist, the mysterious staff member, all have one thing in common – Wisconsin."

John thought to himself. "There is that bulldog in Ken showing up again. That was the way Ken was in sports. He did not have much natural talent in sports, but he would practice something until he got it right. Ken was the most tenacious person John had ever known."

"I will help you out as much as I can, but as I told you, this is not presently considered a crime and my hands are tied in many ways. We have a full case load and it is unlikely that my superiors would allow me to spend time on this," John explained.

Ken was frustrated with his inability to persuade other people to help him with his investigation. No one else seemed to care, and no one was willing to stick their neck out. Because the State of Wisconsin seemed to be at the center of everything, Ken decided to direct his search for answers to that state. He decided to go to Milwaukee to see if he could get some answers.

Ken started searching the name Chad Turnquist. He expected that Mr. Turnquist probably had a cell phone and, like many people, his name would not be in a phone book. He found five people with the name Turnquist and worked out a way to check them out without giving them too much information. He called each number and said he was with an organization that was doing a survey and that each person who completed the survey would receive twenty dollars for their cooperation. In the survey he included questions that would describe Chad Turnquist. Ken had previously asked every staff member at his hospital who had come into contact with Chad Turnquist to tell him everything they could remember about him. This included Dr. Rogers who was being unusually friendly lately.

It was interesting that Dr. Rogers' description of Turnquist was different from the rest of the staff. "What is going on here?" Ken asked himself. "How could Dr. Rogers describe Turnquist as so much shorter and heavier than other staff reported, especially since Dr. Rogers appeared to have had more contact with Turnquist than most of the other staff? Dr. Rogers also said Turnquist had different colored hair than other staff depicted, and that he had a ruddy complexion, which no one else said. John had often mentioned the different descriptions witnesses had of criminals, but could they be this different? Could Dr. Rogers be deliberately trying to mislead me?"

Of the five people Ken called in Wisconsin, one person hung up immediately, one person listened for a minute and hung up, and one person refused to participate. Regarding the two people who agreed to participate, one was much too old and one had been sick for a long time and was restricted to his home.

"Now what do I do?" Ken asked himself. He was beginning to question his motivation. No one else seemed to care. Maybe it was a suicide and everything was legitimate. He had been wrong before, and he was getting tired of banging his head against a wall.

Chapter Fourteen

For the past week Ken had the feeling that someone was following him. When he drove his car, he often saw a blue SUV in his rear view mirror. When he stopped the car, the SUV would drive past. The driver would always turn his head just enough so Ken could not see his face. Ken also thought he saw the SUV parked on the street where he lived.

Ken wondered if he was becoming paranoid. Maybe his involvement in the suicide affected his mind.

Ken shared his feelings about being followed with John at their weekly meeting. That was one of the best things about their relationship. They could tell the other person anything, no matter how weird or personal it was, and they would know that the other person would accept them and keep the information private. Several times, over the years, Ken had shared some very private feelings with John and there was never any evidence that John had told anyone else, not even Sarah.

John and Ken had not met for several weeks because John was working on a new case that took up much of his time. After Ken told John about feeling like he was being followed, John wondered if Ken was getting carried away with his investigation and that it was occupying too much of his time. The same thing had happened to John several times. He would become so engrossed in a case that he could not think about anything else. He knew that his relationship with his family had suffered because of his preoccupation with a case.

Because Ken was such a good friend, John hesitated to suggest that Ken was becoming too involved.

"I'll tell you what I can do," said John. "Try to get the license plate number of the SUV and I will see who it belongs to. How are things going with Becky?" he asked, trying to get Ken to talk about something else.

"We are still dating," responded Ken. He was aware that John was trying to distract him. " I have not had too much spare time lately."

"Sarah still wants to invite you two over for dinner," John said. "That would be great."

On the way home Ken thought about all the time he had spent on the suicide. He realized he had been neglecting his boys and his relationship with Becky. He vowed that he would do something about that, and get his priorities straightened out.

The next day, Ken was back to wondering about the suicide and Chad Turnquist, and how to get more information on him. His thoughts kept going back to Albany Pharmaceuticals.

The company seemed to come up a lot during his investigation. "Maybe I should call Amy, the receptionist, again. Amy has been the most helpful of all the people I talked with," Ken said to himself.

It took several calls to Albany Pharmaceuticals before Ken could reach Amy on her regular shift. When he finally did reach her he thought she seemed more distant and less friendly.

"Are you OK Amy? You seem to be upset," said Ken.

"Who are you?" responded Amy. "I was told not to talk to you and to refer all of your calls to Dr. Benton."

"I don't want to get you in trouble," said Ken. " I just have one more question for you. Could you help me just one more time?"

"I guess so," responded Amy. "But make it quick and don't call me any more."

"Is the name Chad Turnquist familiar to you?" asked Ken. There was a long pause. "Amy, are you still there?"

"Yeah, I'm still here," responded Amy." "Boy, I'm really going to get in trouble if Dr. Benton finds out about this. Dr. Benton talks to someone with a name like that almost every week." "Do you have an address or telephone number for him?" asked Ken.

"No, and I have to go. Please don't call me again," said Amy.

"Finally," Ken said to himself. "A break through after all this time. Maybe it does pay to keep asking questions. I would be a good detective."

"Let's see now," Ken thought to himself. "Mr. Howell, the suicide patient was from Milwaukee. Dr. Benton, the psychiatrist who referred Mr. Howell, is in charge of research and security at a pharmaceutical company in Milwaukee. There may be a connection between Benton and Chad Turnquist, the phantom staff member who found Howell hanging from the light fixture, and who apparently is from Milwaukee. And Dr. Rogers is somehow mixed up in all this. I need to go to Milwaukee to try to make some sense of all this and to either confirm or put to rest my suspicions."

Ken tried to get some paid time off to go to Milwaukee, but his supervisor said no. She could not see how his intentions fit his job description, and she was under the impression that law enforcement had declared the incident a suicide. Ken had three weeks of vacation saved up. He had planned to spend his vacation with Becky and the boys. He decided to take a week off to go to Milwaukee. That would still leave two weeks for the boys and Becky.

To save a couple of days driving to and from Milwaukee, Ken decided to fly and rent a car. The first person Ken decided he would talk with was Dr. Benton. He needed to find out what type of person this Dr. Benton was. Was he really trying to avoid talking to Ken? After flying to Milwaukee, Ken rented a car and found a motel a few miles from Albany Pharmaceuticals. He told the motel clerk he would pay for the room by the day because he did not know how long he would be in town.

In the process of trying to contact Dr. Benton, Ken met Amy, the pleasant and helpful receptionist. Amy was good looking, in her mid twenties. When she realized Ken was the person she had been talking to on the phone, she became very distant and cold, no longer willing to share any information. She refused to have coffee with him and appeared to be afraid to talk to him.

Dr. Benton walked up to the receptionist's desk and Amy turned to work on her computer. "Hello, I'm Alex Benton. I understand you have been trying to talk to me. I'm sorry if I have been hard to reach. I have been very busy, with meeting after meeting."

"Thank you for agreeing to meet with me," responded Ken. "I finally have a few free minutes. Let's go to my office," said Dr. Benton.

"Would you like some coffee Mr. Wold?" asked Dr. Benton.

"Yes, thank you."

"Now what can I do for you?" asked Dr. Benton.

"I am here to follow up on a patient who committed suicide at our hospital," replied Ken. " We have very little information on him and you were the referring psychiatrist."

"What was his name?" asked Dr. Benton. "Thomas Howell," responded Ken.

"I am not familiar with that name," said Dr. Benton. "Even though I only work part time at the hospital, I see a lot of patients when I am on duty. How do you know I treated him?" continued Dr. Benton.

"Dr. Rogers reported that you were the referring psychiatrist and a few weeks after the suicide on August 16th, you sent us a patient summary dated August 19th. In your report you stated that there was no information available on Mr. Howell's background and that you would forward any information that came in," Ken explained.

"Did you get any additional information?" asked Dr. Benton. "No." responded Ken.

"Well then, I guess we were unable to find anything new," stated Dr. Benton "Many of our patients come in off the street with no background information."

"It is important for us to contact family when a patient dies," said Ken. "There may be family members out there who have no idea what happened to Mr. Howell."

"I agree with you on the need to contact family," said Dr. Benton. "I will make it a priority to have the hospital staff follow up on your request and forward any new information to you."

"Isn't it unusual for a person in your position to be seeing new patients at the hospital?" asked Ken.

"Not really," replied Dr. Benton. "I try to stay current in my profession and see as many patients as possible. Sometimes it is difficult, but I believe it is important."

"One more question," said Ken. Do you know anyone by the name of Chad Turnquist?" "No, why do you ask?"

"He was the staff member who found Mr. Howell and it appears that he was from this area," said Ken. He was hoping he did not get Amy in trouble by bringing up the name Turnquist. She was acting differently for a reason.

"Thank you for seeing me," said Ken.

"You are welcome. Call me anytime if you believe I can be helpful in your search for information," responded Dr. Benton, walking with Ken out of the office.

Ken thought he would try to talk to Amy one more time. He thought it would be better if he approached her outside of the office, so he waited in the car until he saw her leave. He watched her get into her car, stop at the grocery store, and go home. Unknown to him, he was being followed by a blue SUV.

Ken parked his car and walked up to Amy's house. He rang the doorbell and Amy opened the door. She said, "Oh no!" and looked up and down the street. She was upset and appeared to be afraid of something.

"I just want to ask you a few questions," Ken said.

"Please leave! I was told not to talk to you. I will lose my job if I am seen talking to you. I have already said too much. Please leave."

Ken realized he was not going to get any more information from Amy. "Just in case you change your mind, here's my card."

Neither Ken nor Amy were aware of the extensive efforts Dr. Benton had taken to be aware of everything that happens at Albany Pharmaceuticals. He had hidden special cameras and microphones throughout the company. He had been recording all the calls that went through the receptionist for the past year. He even knew what the Board of Directors and the CEO talked about outside of the boardroom. Every evening, after the other staff had left for the day, Dr. Benton would review the videos and the conversations he had recorded. He knew what Amy and Ken had talked about, and it was only a matter of time before he would see that Amy was fired. Her probation was just about up, and he would find a way to let her go. Dr. Benton also knew that the Board of Directors, with the exception of the CEO, had a positive impression of him and that he was being considered for the top position in the company. He could not figure out what the CEO had against him. He had to find a way to neutralize William Mattson, the CEO.

When Ken returned home, it was time for him to have a drink with John. Ken told John about his trip to Milwaukee, the meeting with Dr. Benton, and the attempt to talk to Amy.

"She was scared to death." Ken said. "I wish I had your authority to talk to people." They can lie to me, but they would think twice if you were asking the questions. There are so many questions that need to be answered."

"Our hands are often tied too," replied John. "It's not as easy as it looks, especially if no crime has been committed. People are often afraid they might say the wrong things and get themselves in trouble. Many people are afraid they will have to testify in court if they say something, and that is often the truth. We are usually just trying to put clues together to find the right answers."

"So, how are things going with Becky?" John asked. John was trying to change the subject, to get Ken's mind off the suicide, but he was also very interested in his best friend's love life. John asked about Becky every time he and Ken got together, not only because he was interested, but also because he knew his wife, Sarah, would ask him about Becky as soon as he got home. Sarah liked Ken and she wanted the best for him. She was still angry with Diane, Ken's ex-wife, for causing him so much pain.

"Good," replied Ken. "I really like Becky and I think she likes me. I'm thinking about asking her to go away with me for a long weekend. Do you think I am going too fast?" "No," said John, "Go for it."

Chapter Fifteen

Dr. Benton met with Turnquist in a small town outside of Milwaukee. "This Ken Wold is not going to go away," said Benton. "He is going to wreck everything, and we don't know how many people he has been talking to. We are going to have to get rid of him. I didn't think it would go this far," said Benton.

"You mean I have to get rid of him?" asked Turnquist. "Yeah, you," said Benton.

"How about the others?" asked Turnquist. "Let's not get carried away. We have already done too much," replied Benton.

"Rogers seems to be more anxious lately," said Turnquist. "He was upset about what happened to Howell in the first place. He said he never agreed to murder when he approved the transfer to his hospital. He was just trying to do you a favor. He is very concerned about Wold's involvement and he mentioned that Wold had a good friend who is a cop."

"We appear to have scared Amy into being quiet. I don't think she said anything to Wold this last time when he tried to visit her at her home." "I don't think she knows anything," said Benton. "But, just to be sure, I plan to have her fired when her probation is up. We can't have her talking to other people the way she initially talked to Wold."

"Make it look like an accident," said Dr. Benton. "And don't include Rogers in any of your plans."

"This will cost you," replied Turnquist. "What a person will do for money," Dr. Benton said to himself.

Of course, Chad Turnquist is not his real name. His name is James Dugan and very few people know his real name. Experience has taught him not to get close to anyone and to be as anonymous as possible. He was known to a select few as a very dangerous man and as someone who would do anything if the price was right. Dr. Benton became aware of Dugan by accident when he was looking for someone to do a special favor for him which was illegal. Dugan was recommended to Dr. Benton by another ruthless businessman. Dugan and Benton had worked together on several occasions. Even though Benton was afraid of Dugan, he continued to make use of his talents because Dugan had always been successful. Essentially, Dugan did the dirty work for powerful men who exploit others.

Dr. Benton was becoming very good at this part of his job. He had learned how to manipulate politicians and political parties with the use of money. He found he could control a political party or a politician without them even being aware of it. He could just sit back and watch a party run with schemes he dreamed up. He even had some of the talk radio people wrapped around his finger. The old adage, "Follow the money" was certainly true.

Dr. Benton thrived in this environment. When he could not manipulate others with money, he had Dugan available to find ways to influence them and to clean things up. Benton was a very ambitious man and there was no limit to his ambitions. He would not let anyone get in his way to become the CEO at Albany Pharmaceuticals and to receive all the perks that go with the position.

James Dugan was extremely careful and precise in his work. He planned everything out very carefully and seldom made a mistake. When a mistake was made, it was usually related to working with other people, and resulted in Dugan having to clean up after the mistake. In fact, in some circles, Dugan was known as the "Cleaner." He would be hired to clean up after someone else botched a job and make sure there were no loose ends. This occasionally resulted in additional people being killed, such as now, with Ken Wold. If Benton and Rogers had done their jobs correctly, Dugan would not have to kill Wold. " At least I am paid well." Dugan said to himself. He was often paid more for cleaning up after others than he was for doing the job himself. Benton was almost as ruthless as Dugan, so he did not have to worry about him. Rogers was another story.

Rogers had a conscience and was a very anxious person, and anxious people make mistakes. Dugan told himself that he needed to keep his eye on Rogers no matter what Benton says. Rogers knew too much and posed a danger to both Dugan and Benton. He might have to get rid of Rogers to protect himself.

Chapter Sixteen

James Dugan prided himself on his ability to make a murder look like a suicide or an accident. That was one reason he was in such demand. So far, he had a perfect record. This guy Wold was getting too close. If he had not stuck his nose in to everything, there would not be any problems. Dugan was glad Benton had approved the hit. Now he was going to get paid for something he would have had to do anyway.

The natural gas explosion leveled Ken's house and heavily damaged several other houses in the neighborhood. The blast killed Ken and injured five of his neighbors. The blast was heard for miles and left a large hole in the ground where Ken's house once stood, scattering debris over several blocks.

John drove up to where Ken's house used to be. Yellow tape was everywhere. Fire department personnel were still trying to put the fire out. What was left of Ken's body had been taken to the morgue. John walked over to talk to the fire inspector, Eric Truscot. "Looks like a gas leak. I'm sorry. I know you and Mr. Wold were good friends."

"Best friends," responded John. "Are you going to find the source of the leak?"

"Yes, I hope so. The investigation has already started. The gas has been turned off, but things are still very hot. It will probably take some time to find the source of the explosion, but Mr. Wold's house appears to be at the center." John walked around the house and through parts of the foundation that were not still burning.

John had been to Ken's house many times and remembered the different rooms, especially the living room where they had watched many ball games together, drinking beer and eating pizza. John thought about Becky and John's sons. "What if they had been with him, " John thought to himself. "I promise you Ken, if this is not an accident, I will never quit looking for your killer."

Chapter Seventeen

Ken's funeral was well attended. Many of the staff from the hospital came, including Dr. Rogers. John had a hard time trying not to cry. Ken had been such a good friend. John came the closest to breaking down when he saw Ken's sons and Becky. Ken had been so excited about his future. John asked the crime lab photographer to take pictures of the crowd and to act like he worked for the newspaper. John had recently read in a police journal about the number of killers who attended their victim's funeral. It was like they were gloating and proud of their work. When John was not busy with his part in the funeral, he walked around the room where people gathered before and after the service, and at the cemetery grave site. He tried to get a look at everyone who attended, fixating strangers in his memory.

James Dugan had always made a point of keeping up with police work and had read the same journal that John read. He was very careful about staying out of pictures and he did not stay long but, as the article suggested, he could not stay away completely. He had to admire his work and, it was just a job, nothing more.

John knew he was getting ahead of himself, assuming that Ken's death was not an accident. It was not unusual for a gas leak to cause an explosion. Still, just as Ken could not get the hospital suicide out of his mind, John had a very strong feeling that the explosion was not an accident.

The investigation into the explosion was in progress and the investigators had not ruled out an accidental leak as the cause. John was good friends with the fire inspector, Eric Truscot, and knew he would conduct a complete and thorough investigation. The problem was that the investigation was taking so long, and John could not start his own investigation until Truscot's was completed.

Very few people were aware of Ken and John's weekly meetings at the Riverside Inn and that John was very much aware of Ken's suspicions about the apparent suicide at the hospital. John thought to himself that if Ken was on to something, he must have gotten some people very upset, enough to have him killed. John decided to write down everything he could remember about his conversations with Ken, including the smallest bits of information that probably meant nothing now, but could mean a lot later on. John worked very closely with the investigators, almost to the point where they resented his attempt to be helpful. He irritated them with his constant questions. They put up with John's behavior because they were aware of how close he was to Ken, and they would have done the same thing if they were in his shoes.

Eric Truscot confirmed that the explosion was caused by a gas leak.

He said a small crack in the gas pipe going to the furnace appeared to be the cause of the leak. It was strange that the leak occurred because there was a tag on the furnace stating that it had recently been inspected. John asked him who would be responsible for checking the gas pipes and Truscot told him it was the gas company. He told John he was taking the defective pipe into his shop to take a closer look at the crack.

John went to the gas company and asked for the records of the inspection recently completed at Ken's house. He was given the records and the name of the person who did the inspection, Patrick Small. John asked the receptionist if he could speak to Mr. Small.

He was told that Mr. Small was currently conducting another inspection. He made an appointment to speak to Mr. Small the next day. When John met with Mr. Small, the inspector said he was surprised when he heard about the explosion. He said Ken requested an inspection a few weeks ago because he wanted to make sure his children would be safe when they stayed overnight at his house. John thought that was just like Ken, to ask for an inspection. Ken was a stickler for detail, especially when it came to his children. Mr. Small said Ken had heard about a similar explosion in another state in which some children were injured. He went on to say he had checked the gas line very carefully and he could not find anything wrong. He said it is possible that he missed something, but it is doubtful.

John was very close to concluding that the explosion was not an accident. The only thing left was confirmation from the fire inspector that it was a homicide. After that, he had to persuade his supervisor to assign him to the case.

"We have determined that the recent explosion which killed one person and injured five others was not an accident." Eric Truscot reported to the public. "A small pipe that leads to the furnace in the house owned by the victim, Ken Wold, was cut with a saw. This is now a criminal investigation. While the fire investigation has been progressing, there has been a parallel investigation focusing on individuals who may have been responsible, if an accidental cause was ruled out. At this time we cannot provide any information on possible suspects."

John's supervisor, Lieutenant Lynn Shafer, has been with the police department for twenty years. She worked her way up the career ladder the hard way, having to contend with the constant implications about women in law enforcement. She took every possible training course, from karate to the illegal manufacture of drugs. Her karate instructor told her that if she could conquer karate, it would change her life. He was right. She was very confident about being able to handle herself physically in any situation, and her confident feelings permeated every facet of her life. She had worked undercover for two years and held an M.A. degree in public administration. Lieutenant Shafer had held John's position for ten years before she was promoted.

"Are you sure you want to take this on?" Lieutenant Shafer asked. "I know that Ken was your best friend. You might be too close to the case to be objective."

"I realize that, and I understand your concerns, but Ken and I talked about everything almost every week, especially his suspicions about the apparent suicide at the hospital. No one else could possibly have the information that I have."

"Well, I will assign you to the case, but I will not hesitate to pull you off if I think your closeness to Ken is affecting your objectivity. And remember, we have a very limited budget, so don't get carried away."

Chapter Eighteen

John remembered that Ken told him he kept a record of his investigation related to the suicide in a journal in his office. Ken said he wrote in the journal every week. John thought that if he could get his hands on that kind of information it would save him many hours. He asked Ken's supervisor if he could borrow the journal. Mrs. Carlson was surprised at the request because she had assumed Ken was not getting anywhere with his suspicions. She was also shocked to hear that the explosion had been declared a homicide and that Ken was the intended victim. She could not understand why anyone would want to kill such a wonderful man.

"I helped to clean out Ken's office and box up his personal things," she said. "I don't remember seeing anything that looked like a journal. You need to understand that if we do find a journal, it may contain privileged information about other patients."

"I understand."

Mrs. Carlson was not surprised to hear that Ken had kept a record of his investigation because he was known for paying attention to detail. "When we went through the office I was surprised to find it was not as neat as I remembered. Ken always kept a neat office. The room looked messy and lacked organization," she said.

"Maybe you weren't the first person to go through the office." John said. "I don't know what reason someone would have to go through Ken's papers." "I do," replied John.

John and Mrs. Carlson opened all the boxes and went through the room again. They could not find anything related to Ken's investigation of the suicide. This was very irritating to John because now he would have to start all over, relying on his memory of everything Ken told him about his investigation. "Who else would have a key to Ken's office?" asked John.

"Several people, janitors, supervisory staff, and doctors all have master keys to almost every room in the hospital."

"So Dr. Rogers would have access to Ken's office?" John asked. "Yes, why do you ask?" "If I remember correctly, Dr. Rogers was a key person in the suicide."

Chapter Nineteen

John was sitting in his office writing notes to himself, trying to remember everything Ken told him about the suicide. The more Ken had looked into the suicide incident, the more questions he came up with. The primary people Ken talked about were the patient who committed suicide, Dr. Rogers, the temporary staff person who found the patient, the doctor from Wisconsin who referred the patient, and a receptionist called Amy.

"Ken must have gotten someone very upset and worried." John said to himself. "If the suicide and Ken's murder are connected, he must have been on to something, the importance of which not even Ken knew"

Although the suicide and the individuals involved would be John's primary targets in his investigation, he knew that he needed to look into every possibility. He could not overlook anything or anybody. Sometimes the smallest discrepancy had led to his solving major crimes. First, John needed to talk to Ken's girlfriend, Becky, and his ex- wife, Diane. John did not believe there would be any connection to Becky or Diane, but he needed to check it out. He also had to look into all of Ken's work and off-work activities, to rule out all other possibilities.

"How is the investigation going on the death of your friend?" asked Lieutenant Shafer. "Slow," responded John. "I checked out Ken's ex-wife and girlfriend, but I could not come up with any reason why they might be involved, such as a jealous husband or ex- boyfriend. There was an insurance policy, but all of the money goes to Ken's children.

The ex-wife inherited a lot of money recently. Ken and his ex-wife got along amazingly well, considering the circumstances. They shared custody of the children. I have known Diane since we were in high school and she has always been pretty level headed. The one thing that currently stands out is Ken's investigation of the apparent suicide at the hospital and the absence of a journal Ken said he kept in his office."

"A journal?" asked Lieutenant Shafer.

"Yeah, Ken was a stickler for detail and he told me he was keeping a record of his investigation. His supervisor, Mrs. Carlson, and I went through his office very carefully and we could not find a thing related to the suicide. Mrs. Carlson stated that the office was messy, with papers all over, when she first started to box up his things. She said this was not like Ken. His office was normally neat and organized."

"So you think someone went through his office before Mrs. Carlson had a chance to do so?" asked Lieutenant Shafer.

"Possibly, it would make sense, but only if Ken was on to something and the suicide was really a homicide."

"Now that is the first time I have heard that," said Lieutenant Shafer.

"Our investigators, the coroner, and the doctors at the hospital have all gone on record that it was strictly a suicide."

"It would not be the first time something like that has happened. Remember that case five years ago? It was seen as an accident until more evidence proved otherwise. The more Ken looked into things, and the more people he talked to, the more suspicious he became. That may have been the reason he was killed, he was getting too close to the truth."

"Keep me informed about the investigation, especially if you are going to conclude that the suicide was a murder," said Lieutenant Shafer. "The Chief of Police will want to know too. It could become very political."

Chapter Twenty

"Now where do I go from here." John asked himself. " I think I will begin by talking to everyone Ken mentioned in our conversations. When you shake the tree, you never know what will fall out. I will start with Dr. Rogers since he was an integral part of Ken's investigation and he is the only person Ken talked with who lives in town." John called Dr. Rogers to make an appointment and talked to his secretary. An appointment was made for a week from the day John called. The day before the scheduled appointment, John received a call from Dr. Rogers' secretary, changing the appointment to the next week. It happened a second time and John said that was enough. He had Dr. Rogers picked up and brought to the police station.

Dr. Rogers was extremely angry about being brought to the police station, ranting about his rights, the embarrassment of being picked up at the hospital, and how his patients were suffering with him being gone. John let Dr. Rogers sit in the interview room until he calmed down. John was very much aware of the mental anguish people experienced when they had to sit alone in the interview room, especially when they were guilty. They wondered how much you know, and what they should and should not say. The more they sat, the more they worried. Dr. Benton had instructed Dr. Rogers to postpone the appointments with John as long as he could. Dr. Benton told him John would probably think Dr. Rogers was too busy and would give up trying to contact him. That did not work. "Why did I get involved in this in the first place?" Dr. Rogers asked himself. "I should have turned Benton down when he wanted to transfer that person."

"Hello Dr. Rogers," John said as he walked into the interview room. "I am sorry we had to bring you down to the precinct, but it seemed to be the only way I could get you to talk with me. You canceled my appointments several times. Like you, we are busy too, and cancelled appointments waste our time."

"What is this all about?" Dr. Rogers asked angrily. I have patients to see." He appeared to be very anxious and nervous.

"As you know, we are investigating the murder of Ken Wold."

"What does that have to do with me?"

"What you may not know is that Ken and I often talked about his interest in the suicide of one of your patients, Thomas Howell. Ken's murder may have something to do with the apparent suicide," John said.

"I can't see how the two are connected."

"That is what we are trying to figure out and we were hoping you could help us. Your name came up frequently during our conversations.

I also need to tell you that this conversation is being recorded, and that I will very likely be speaking to you in the future. I am just beginning my investigation and I probably will have more questions. I am determined to get to the bottom of this. If you are involved in this in any way, and I find out you were lying to me, I will not hesitate to put you in jail," John explained.

John was deliberately trying to intimidate Dr. Rogers. This was just the beginning of John's attempt to stir things up. "As I understand it, you admitted Mr. Howell and were his primary psychiatrist."

"Yes, that's right, and, I don't like your attitude. You are treating me as if I were a criminal."

"Who referred Mr. Howell?" John continued.

"Dr. Alex Benton, a friend of mine who works part time at Albany Hospital in Milwaukee," responded Dr. Rogers.

"Why would he send a patient such a long distance?" asked John.

"Sometimes treatment facilities are full of patients and the referring hospital has to work hard to find openings," said Dr. Rogers. "In this new system we have, there are times when we have to send patients a long distance to get treated."

"Isn't it more complicated to send patients out of state, both financially and legally?"

"It depends. If the patient is on a certain type of insurance, it is not a problem."

"What type of insurance did Mr. Howell have?"

"I'm not really sure. We were trying to work that out when Mr. Howell committed suicide."

"What was your diagnosis of Mr. Howell?"

"Dr. Benton made the initial diagnosis of schizophrenia and I agreed with the diagnosis," replied Dr. Rogers. "Dr. Benton also prescribed the initial medication which I continued when Mr. Howell arrived." "How did Mr. Howell look to you when he arrived?" asked John.

"He was very paranoid, talking about aliens being after him. He was also very drowsy, slurring his words, and it was hard to understand him."

"Did Mr. Howell appear to be suicidal to you?" "No, if I thought he was suicidal, I would have assigned a staff member to watch him. I was very surprised when I heard he had committed suicide, but it is not unusual. We have several suicides or suicidal attempts every year.

"What do you know about the staff person who found Mr. Howell?" asked John.

"His name was Chad Turnquist," said Dr. Rogers. " He was new and I did not get to know him."

"You were the last person to see Mr. Turnquist before he resigned. Is that correct?"

"I think so. I really don't know if I was the last person. Mr. Turnquist was extremely upset and wanted to quit soon after he found Mr. Howell," replied Dr. Rogers.

"Did you encourage Mr. Turnquist to leave?"

"Some people are just not cut out for this work. A lot of bad things happen in mental hospitals and some people can't take it."

"What did Mr. Turnquist look like?"

"He was about average height and weight, nothing really outstanding." "What color was his hair?" "I really can't remember, brown I think."

"Thank you for speaking to me." said John. "I know you are a very busy man and I apologize for having you brought down here."

"Your attitude was very offensive and accusatory. I am going to make a formal complaint to the Chief of Police. Can I go now?"

"Yes. We will have someone drive you back to the hospital." "That will not be necessary," responded Dr. Rogers. "I will find my own way back."

Chapter Twenty-one

As soon as he got back to the hospital, Dr. Rogers called Dr. Benton on his drop phone, which very few people were aware of or had access to. Two of those people were Dr. Rogers and James Dugan. "I talked to that detective today," said Dr. Rogers.

"I thought I told you to avoid him." demanded Dr. Benton.

"It's hard to avoid someone when he has you picked up at the hospital and brought to the police station. It was embarrassing to have two cops come to your office and escort you to the police car in front of staff and patients. Why did you have to kill Wold? It just made things worse. They have declared the gas explosion was a homicide. Your buddy Turnquist, or whatever his name is, really screwed up this time," said Dr. Rogers. "And, did you know that the police detective in charge of the investigation and Wold were good friends? This detective is like a bulldog. Wold must have talked to him about his suspicions before he was killed. What a mess."

"Calm down," said Dr. Benton. "It will be hard for the detective to conduct his investigation without Wold's journal. It was a good thing you found it."

"I was against killing Howell and killing Wold was a complete surprise. How can you do this? We aren't killers," said Dr. Rogers.

"We are now, and you don't realize how much money was at stake if we did not take care of Howell, just remember, you are in this thing up to your neck. Keep your mouth shut and give out as little information as possible. In the meantime, I will tighten up things around here," concluded Dr. Benton.

Dr. Benton was getting a little anxious himself, wondering if he had gone too far. He decided to give Dugan a call on his drop phone. "I thought you didn't make mistakes."

Dr. Benton said. "What do you mean?" asked Dugan.

"The gas explosion has been declared a homicide and the detective in charge of the investigation was a close friend of Wold's."

"I knew Wold had drinks with someone at the Riverside Inn, but I did not know who it was. Do you want me to take care of him?" asked Dugan.

"No, you have done enough already. It's time to back off. You had better lay low for a while. Take a long vacation."

"I have a couple of jobs to do. I will take off after that," Dugan said.

Chapter Twenty-two

John tried to remember everything Ken said about his investigation of the suicide. He wondered if he should request that the case be reopened. He had to admit that he did not pay close attention to Ken's discussion of the incident at the hospital because it appeared to be a suicide and all the responsible professionals had signed off on the case. Ken was really the only person who had serious questions about the suicide and maybe he was correct. When they were discussing the suicide, John remembered thinking that he had enough cases to work on and he did not have the time to get involved in another investigation. Now, it was different. Ken's murder had changed everything. Ken was his best friend and he was not going to rest until he solved Ken's murder. Whoever killed Ken had made a terrible mistake and they were going to pay for it.

John reviewed everything he knew about the suicide at the hospital and Ken's murder. He needed more evidence to convince Lieutenant Shafer to open the suicide case and to allow him to go to Milwaukee. He had already talked to Dr. Rogers and John was convinced Dr. Rogers was hiding something. John decided he would put Dr. Rogers on hold for a while and get back to him later. The only other leads are the patient who committed suicide and the staff member who found him. " I will check on this Dr. Benton who referred the patient when and if I get to Milwaukee," John said to himself.

"These confidentiality issues are a real problem sometimes," John remarked to his supervisor. "I realize they are necessary in order to protect people, but they make it very difficult to get information."

"Yes," responded Lieutenant Shafer. "By the way, the Chief received a complaint from Dr. Rogers about your having him picked up at the hospital and your attitude during the interview. Lucky for you, the Chief has great respect for you and your ability to conduct yourself in an appropriate manner. He understands that you probably had a good reason to do what you did, but he is concerned, as I am, that you may be too close to the case."

"I was a little rough on him, but, as you well know, people make mistakes when you get them upset. I will be more careful in the future."

"You will have a hard time finding a judge who will sign a search warrant and allow you to go through patient's and staff member's files," Lieutenant Shafer said.

"I agree," said John. "I may talk to Judge Seagram about the situation just to see how much information I need."

"Good luck," said Lieutenant Shafer.

"Now let me get this straight," said Judge Seagram. "You want me to open a closed case so you can look at the files of a patient and a staff member."

"I believe there is a connection between the murder of Ken Wold and the apparent suicide of a patient at the hospital," said John. "Ken suspected that the suicide was really a murder and he was doing his own investigation. I think he was getting too close to the truth, and was killed for that reason. It may have something to do with a pharmaceutical company in Milwaukee."

"Didn't the coroner, the hospital staff, and the police department sign off on the suicide?" asked Judge Seagram. Sharon Seagram has been a district court judge for ten years and is widely known as a judge who is fair and who is willing to listen to other people without making snap judgments. That was the reason John picked her to talk to. They had worked together on several cases in the past, and John was very impressed with her common sense and legal talent.

"Yes, right now it is more of a feeling, based on all the things Ken said before he was killed, and the few conversations I have had since the case was assigned to me."

"I'm sorry John. I think you are a great detective, but you need more and better information in order for me to open the case and allow you to review confidential information. What you have brought me so far is based on your hunches and that is not enough. Based on past experiences with you, I know your hunches are usually correct, but I need more than that to rule in your favor. Bring me more and better information,"

Judge Seagram concluded. "I know it will only make your job harder, but knowing you, you will find a way to make it work."

John felt like he was butting his head against a wall, but this was not the first time he had ever felt this way, and it would not be the last. Many people would just give up, but not him. The more obstacles that were placed in his way, the harder he worked. He needed to go back to the explosion, talk to more people, and find enough evidence to persuade Judge Seagram to open the suicide case.

Chapter Twenty-three

The first stop was Mrs. Helms, a retired widow who lived across the street from Ken. Luckily, she was not injured in the blast because she happened to be in her basement. She had reported to the investigators that she saw a Compton Energy van parked in front of Ken's house the same day of the explosion. She was now living with a daughter on the north side of town, waiting for the insurance company to contact her. She had lived in the house for forty years, raised her children in the house, and saw her husband die of a stroke in the living room. She planned on rebuilding the house. She was not ready to leave the neighborhood and live elsewhere.

John rang the doorbell and Mrs. Helms answered the door. Her daughter and son-in-law were at work and the grandchildren were in school. John introduced himself to Mrs. Helms. She invited him into the house and offered him a cup of coffee. "I am investigating the murder of Mr. Wold," John said.

"I was shocked when it was reported in the newspaper that you thought it was a murder. I thought it was a gas line explosion. You hear about that happening every once in a while.

Poor Mr. Wold. Why would anyone want to kill such a nice man? I hope you catch the person who did this. I lock my doors all the time now. How do you know it was murder?" Mrs. Helms asked.

"The investigator who checked the gas line noticed a small cut in the line that goes to the furnace and the gas company had just inspected the line a few weeks before the explosion. It was fortunate that the investigator was able to locate the cut line. Usually, it is impossible to find the exact cause of such large explosions," said John. "I am surprised the inspector could find anything. The explosion was so big and the entire house seemed to have disappeared."

What if the boys had been with him?" Mrs. Helms said. "What a terrible thing to happen, and in my neighborhood. We have never had anything like that happen before. It was such a peaceful place."

"Is there anything you can remember about that day? Anything that was unusual?" John asked.

"Nothing that I can think of," responded Mrs. Helms. "I remember seeing a man from the gas company get out of his truck and walk right into the house. At the time I thought it was strange, for him to walk in without knocking, but I assumed Mr. Wold left a key for him."

"What did the man look like?"

"I remember thinking what a fine looking man he was," replied Mrs. Helms. "He was tall, like you, slim, very athletic looking. He had light colored hair. I remember the hair because the wind blew his hat off."

"You did not tell the investigators about the color of the man's hair when you first talked to them. Is there any reason you are able to remember the color of his hair now?" John asked.

"I was very upset that day. I almost got killed. There was so much noise, with all the sirens, and so many people around."

"I understand. I am not trying to give you a hard time. I am just trying to get as much accurate information as I can. In this business, you can't get enough information. So, to summarize, you are sure you saw a tall, well built man with light hair get out of a gas company vehicle and enter the house."

"Yes," responded Mrs. Helms.

Why didn't I get that information before? John asked himself. Now I'm going to have to go back and find out what Thomas Howell and Chad Turnquist looked like. I can't trust anything Dr. Rogers told me. Sometimes I wonder if I am loosing my edge in this job.

John visited every house in the neighborhood in which people were still living. He also tried to talk to those who had been temporarily displaced because of the damage to their home. Mrs. Helms was the only person who reported something new and different.

Compton Energy had reported that one of its vans was stolen the night before the explosion. The next day, the van was found parked on one of the side streets. When it was discovered that the van was missing, Compton Energy was slow in reporting the theft, thinking it was probably kids going for a joy ride. It was two days before the investigators tied the stolen van to the explosion. By that time, several employees had used the van and there were no strange fingerprints. John thought the killer had probably wiped the van clean of fingerprints anyway.

John decided that his next move would be to talk to staff at the hospital again and to make sure he got good descriptions of Thomas Howell and Chad Turnquist. The first person he contacted was Jane Carlson, the Social Services Director, and Ken's supervisor.

"Thank you for agreeing to see me again Mrs. Carlson," John said. "I need to tell you that at the present time I am just investigating Ken's murder, not the suicide at the hospital. I have not received approval from my supervisor or the judge to reopen the suicide. Having said that, the topic of the suicide may come up in our discussion." John said, smiling.

"I understand."

"I asked Judge Seagram to open the suicide case, but she said I did not have enough evidence to do so. I am interested in the suicide because Ken was so involved in investigating it and kept me informed about his progress. Besides, the suicide is the only thing I have come up with that would suggest further inquiry. As you remember, when we looked through Ken's office we could not find his notes on the suicide and I am sure he told me he was keeping a journal. Not having that journal has resulted in my starting over in my investigation," John explained.

"I know Judge Seagram. We are in a book club together and she has been very helpful to me in the past regarding patient issues," said Mrs. Carlson. "I am very upset about Ken's murder and the more I think about it, the more I want to help you, even to the point of stretching the legal issues. You know more about the law than I do, so you will have to stop me when I step over the line. I looked for Chad Turnquist's file, but I can't find it. Someone may have taken it," reported Mrs. Carlson.

"You can't believe how good it is to hear that, and to have someone on my side," said John. "I am really having a hard time getting good information, but I refuse to give up. Isn't it interesting that Ken's journal and Turnquist's file are both missing? I would be willing to bet that Mr. Howell's chart will be hard to find also. It is those kind of things that add up and point the investigation in a certain direction. It also suggests that a staff member in the hospital who has access to all this information may be involved. Currently, Turnquist's personnel file is off limits, according to Judge Seagram, as is Howell's chart. If we can get more evidence, we might be able to talk Judge Seagram into opening the suicide case again."

"Tell me what you need and I will try to help," said Mrs. Carlson. "Maybe I could learn more about Howell and Turnquist if you could get me the names and telephone numbers of all the staff who were on duty when both Howell and Turnquist were on the unit," John said.

"That should not be too hard. Staff usually work on the same shift together. The number of people to contact could be quite large since we are talking about three eight hour shifts during a twenty four hour period. We may have a confidentiality problem. Is that a violation of confidentiality?" asked Mrs. Carlson.

"It may be." John said, while checking over his notes. "We may not be able to use whatever we learn in court, but I think it is worth the risk. It should give us some leads we can follow up on."

"I like it when you say we. It means I am helping to find Ken's killer," said Mrs. Carlson.

After he left the meeting with Mrs. Carlson, John felt better about the case. He found at least one person who wants to help and is willing to stretch the rules to get information.

Now he needs to find a few more people like Mrs. Carlson who are on his side and who are willing to help. That seems to be the way most investigations work. You just keep digging and talking to people until things start to make sense and fall in line. That is probably what happened to Ken. He would not give up on his investigation and he learned too much, John said to himself.

Several days after the meeting with Mrs. Carlson, John received a list of names and telephone numbers of staff who worked on the hospital unit when Howell and Turnquist were there. Mrs. Carlson also included dates and times the staff were scheduled to work on the unit in the future. She had asterisks marked next to the names of staff she thought would be the most cooperative and helpful. John thought she must have had help getting the information from other staff that wanted to help. Mrs. Carlson really had nothing to do with staff work assignments except for staff that reported directly to her.

Chapter Twenty-four

Pat Koch was the first person on the hospital staff that John talked to. She was one of the people Mrs. Carlson thought would be cooperative. Mrs. Koch was close to retirement and had been the lead nurse on the unit for twenty four years. John remembered seeing her crying at Ken's funeral.

John arranged to meet with Mrs. Koch at the hospital. Mrs. Koch took John to the conference room. On the way to the conference room they passed Dr. Rogers coming out of his office. He looked like he was surprised to see John, but did not say anything, moving quickly down the hallway. John was glad Dr. Rogers saw him. John had the feeling that Dr. Rogers had not been truthful with him and that somehow he was involved in the investigation John was conducting. John just could not figure out how or why Dr. Rogers was involved. John wanted Dr. Rogers to be worried and upset. That is often when a lot of people make mistakes. "I would like to get a copy of his telephone calls, "John said to himself.

"Would you like some coffee?" asked Mrs. Koch.

"Yes, thank you," replied John.

"Jane Carlson told me you might be contacting me. She wanted to assure me that I had not done anything wrong, and that you were a nice person to talk to. She said you were investigating the murder of Ken Wold. Is that what you want to talk about?" Mrs. Koch asked.

"Yes. Several months ago, you had a suicide on the unit and Ken was not sure it was a suicide. He had been doing his own investigation and that may be the reason he was killed." "The two incidents may or may not be connected. That is what I am trying to determine. Primarily, I want to ask you some questions about the suicide," John explained.

"Well, there may be some confidentiality issues and I may not be able to answer all of your questions."

"I understand," said John. "I have repeatedly run into the confidentiality issue during my investigation."

"I really liked Ken and I would like to help you as much as I can. He was a good friend and a good social worker. He was always teasing me about my retirement plans."

"He was my friend too. In fact, he was my best friend."

John continued with the discussion. "As I indicated, I am looking into every facet of Ken's life prior to his death, trying to find a connection between his murder and other parts of his life. He was assigned to this unit and he was in the process of looking into the apparent suicide of Thomas Howell."

"Yes, I remember him talking to me about the suicide. He asked me a lot of questions. I thought his interest was rather strange because it appeared to be a clear case of suicide. Maybe I missed something. I was on duty the evening of the suicide." Mrs. Koch said.

"What do you remember about Thomas Howell? Don't leave anything out. Sometimes the smallest thing can lead to further questions. And, as I said, I understand about confidentiality. It drives me crazy sometimes, but I do understand the need for it."

"The first thing that comes to mind is Dr. Rogers informing me that a new patient was coming to our unit and to call him when the patient arrived," Mrs. Koch said. " I thought it was a little unusual because Dr. Rogers usually goes home and I call him at home when a new patient is admitted to the unit. This time he stayed in his office. Another thing that was unusual was that we have an admission policy and new patients are usually admitted to another unit and transferred to our unit after they are examined by the admitting psychiatrist. We do not question a psychiatrist's decision about patients because they are in charge of patient care. However, Mr. Howell's admission did not follow policy."

"Mr. Howell arrived about 7:00 p.m.," Mrs. Koch continued. "He arrived in an ambulance from Albany Hospital in Milwaukee. I thought it was strange because we are a long way from Milwaukee and there must be numerous treatment facilities closer to Milwaukee. It is also unusual to get a patient from out of state. There was something else that was different."

"Mr. Howell's arrival by ambulance was a little strange too. Patients usually arrive in a police car or are accompanied by a social worker. It is much more expensive to use an ambulance."

John was having a hard time keeping up with Mrs. Koch with his note taking so he asked her if he could tape the interview. He was feeling very positive about the interview because Mrs. Koch had a good memory and she was willing to talk to him.

Mrs. Koch agreed to the use of the tape recorder and continued with the interview. "I called Dr. Rogers as soon as the patient arrived. Dr. Rogers was unusually concerned about every facet of Mr. Howell's hospitalization. He picked the room to which Mr. Howell was assigned, insisted he not have a roommate, and even picked the staff member who would conduct the patient orientation. All the staff, including myself, went along with Dr. Rogers' requests because he gets angry when his orders are not followed, or when a staff member questions his orders. That reminds me. Ken was one of the few staff on the unit who was not afraid to question Dr. Rogers and he seemed to enjoy it when he got Dr. Rogers angry. When Mr. Howell arrived he could hardly stand up. He was on a heavy dose of medication and Dr. Rogers continued the prescription. Mr. Howell tried to talk, but it was impossible to understand him. When one of the nurses questioned the dosage, Dr. Rogers became upset. Dr. Rogers made sure his directions were followed before he left for the night. Mr. Howell was very drowsy and had a difficult time eating. I really can't see how he was able to hang himself. If he could not stand up without help, how could he have gone through the process of hanging himself?"

"Would you describe the patient?" John asked.

"If he stood up straight, I would say he was five feet and eight or nine inches tall," responded Mrs. Koch. "He looked to be about 45 years old. He was a little paunchy. His dark hair had some grey in it. He smiled once and I remember saying to myself that he had a nice smile. Oh yes, he seemed to have a twitch in his right eye, kind of like a blink. It could have been caused by all the medication he was on."

"What do you know about Chad Turnquist, the staff member who found Mr. Howell hanging?"

"That was another strange thing." "Apparently, Dr. Rogers had something to do with Mr. Turnquist's hiring and leaving so quickly. That is the rumor anyway. Staff are always gossiping and that is the story going around."

"What did Turnquist look like?"

"The female staff started talking about him as soon as he arrived on the unit. It was the day before Howell was admitted. He was very good looking. He was tall, had light sandy looking hair, and had a great build. He looked like he was one of those people who work out on a regular basis. We were happy to see him on the unit for several reasons."

"One reason was that we were short of staff. Another reason was that it is always nice to have a big strong man working on the unit to help control the more aggressive patients. You never have enough strong bodies when it comes to holding down a patient who is acting out. The flu was going around among the staff and the patients, and the personnel department was running out of temporary staff they could call on. When Dr. Rogers recommended Mr. Turnquist, the personnel department jumped on the chance to hire him on a temporary basis," continued Mrs. Koch.

"Dr. Rogers recommended Mr. Turnquist?"

"Yes, Dr. Rogers apparently knew him from a previous job." This was surprising information to John because Dr. Rogers claimed he did not know Turnquist prior to his being hired.

"What was Mr. Turnquist like?"

"He was very quiet and did not socialize with the other staff. We thought he was just shy. He spent a lot of time with Mr. Howell after he arrived. In fact, it was Dr. Rogers who insisted that Mr. Turnquist be assigned to watch Mr. Howell," reported Mrs. Koch.

"Were you on duty when Mr. Howell was found?" "No, I had completed my shift and I was not scheduled to return to work for several days."

"Is there anything, even the smallest thing you can think of that stands out as being different during the time period around Mr. Howell's suicide?"

"No, I think I have told you everything I know." replied Mrs. Koch.

"Thank you for talking to me. You have given me some good and new information I can use in my investigation. We will see where it takes me. Please don't hesitate to call me if you remember something you may have overlooked during our conversation. Here is my card."

"I am glad I was able to be helpful. I will call you if I remember anything new," replied Mrs. Koch.

John talked with several other staff on the unit and they confirmed Mrs. Koch's statements. John felt the need to ask Dr. Rogers about his paying special attention to Mr. Howell and his denial about knowing Turnquist. John decided to wait until he had more information. Now, he was sure that Dr. Rogers was hiding something. He remembered his supervisor telling him that interviewing was an art, and that timing was everything. It was time to plan a visit to Milwaukee.

Chapter Twenty-five

Dr. Rogers called Dr. Benton in Milwaukee. "That cop is nosing around the unit and talking to staff. He is not going to give up on his investigation."

"Take it easy. Don't get upset," replied Dr. Benton. "And, don't act like you are disturbed. It would really make the detective suspicious if you act like he is getting to you and you are guilty of something. Keep me informed about everything that happens. Don't call me on this line anymore. I am going to get another drop phone and I will give you the number to call," said Dr. Benton.

"Just don't kill anyone else," Dr. Rogers said. "We are in enough trouble already."

John was talking to his supervisor, Lieutenant Shafer. " I have to go to Milwaukee." John said. "Everything points to that area as being the place where it all started. Ken mentioned the names of a few people in Milwaukee when we were discussing his investigation. I remember some of the names and that is where I plan to start. I wish I had his journal. That would really help me out. The absence of the journal is just more evidence that he was onto something. Someone must have thought it was important enough to break into his office and go through his papers."

"You are really sticking your neck out, looking into a closed case. The Chief of Police would not approve of your spending so much time on this. Somehow, you need to tie the suicide and Ken's death together."

"That's what I am trying to do."

"Make sure you check in with the local authorities. You will need them to be on your side, not putting obstacles in your way."

As soon as John could get a few days off from his other work, he left for Milwaukee. The first thing he did after arriving in Milwaukee was to contact the local police department.

John asked to speak to the precinct captain, Jackson Arnold, and told him about the investigation.

"Albany Pharmaceuticals is one of the biggest employers in Milwaukee and they have a lot of political clout," said Captain Arnold. "Be careful in your investigation and I better not receive a call from the Chief of Police about you. In fact, I think I will call the Chief now and tell him about you being in the area. I want to know immediately if anything related to the investigation includes Albany Pharmaceuticals."

"I will tread very lightly and I will keep you closely informed about my investigation."

"Don't get me wrong. We support your investigation. We heard about the murder and we will try to be helpful. Just to be on the safe side, give me the name and telephone number of your supervisor so I can check you out."

Captain Arnold called Lieutenant Shafer as soon as John left his office. He told her about John's visit. " John is one of my best detectives and I can assure you he will be careful and will act in an appropriate manner. There is only one thing that bothers me," said Lieutenant Shafer.

"What is that?"

"The murder victim was John's best friend. They go way back to elementary school and Ken was John's best man and godfather to John's children," said Lieutenant Shafer.

"Thanks for telling me that. I will call you if I or the Chief have any questions."

Captain Arnold called the Chief of Police and told him about John's investigation. The Chief, Duane Erickson, said he was not surprised. He said he had received several reports of misconduct on the part of security staff at Albany Pharmaceuticals. There was not enough hard evidence to begin an investigation, but the Chief said he thought it would only be a matter of time before something came up. He said he did not know how deep the problem went in the organization. "Keep me informed about everything that happens," said Chief Erickson "Albany Pharmaceuticals has a lot of positive history in this town and we have to proceed with caution and be sure of every step we take."

Chapter Twenty-six

John walked up to the receptionist desk at Albany Pharmaceuticals and asked to speak to Amy. He knew this was a long shot, but he did not know Amy's last name. He just remembered Ken talking about a receptionist whose name was Amy when he was telling John about his trip to Milwaukee. "Amy Crane?" asked the receptionist. "She does not work here any longer. She left about two months ago."

"Do you have an address or telephone number for her?"

"No I don't. I couldn't give it to you anyway. I am not allowed to give out any information on past or present employees."

"Who could I talk to in order to get the information?" John asked, trying to establish the line of authority.

"That would be Dr. Benton, the head of security. He is the only person who could give you that information," the receptionist said. " There's that name again," John said to himself.

There were twenty five Cranes in the Milwaukee telephone book and John was in the process of calling all twenty five. When he got to number fourteen he found Amy.

"Mrs. Crane, I am a detective with the Lawrence Minnesota Police Department. May I ask you a few questions?"

"I'm not married. What do you want to know and why are you calling me?

"Did you ever work for Albany Pharmaceuticals as a receptionist?"

"Yes, I worked there for almost six months and they let me go when my probation was completed. I think they were trying to save money because I was supposed to get a raise after I completed my probation period."

"Could we meet someplace and talk?"

"I don't know," Amy said suspiciously. "I guess so."

"It's about a case I am working on. Could we meet in a public place where you would feel more comfortable, such as a restaurant?" asked John.

"O.K., how about Mannings on second street, 1:00 p.m., and bring some money because I'm hungry. I will be wearing a black skirt with a red blouse."

John walked into Mannings restaurant and immediately spotted Amy. Her blouse was a bright red. She was a pretty girl and probably did not have a problem attracting men. "Amy? I'm Detective Davis. Thank you for agreeing to meet with me. Would you like to order? You said you were going to be hungry." Amy smiled and ordered a salad and John ordered a sandwich.

After a few minutes of small talk about the weather, in an attempt to relieve Amy of any fears she might have, John moved on to investigative questions. "Do you remember talking to a man called Ken Wold?" John asked. "He said you were very nice to him and you were helpful in his investigation."

"I remember him very clearly."

"He almost got me fired. Dr. Benton, one of the big shots at Albany Pharmaceuticals who was in charge of security, got very angry at me after I talked to Mr. Wold. I had never seen him get that angry. Dr. Benton was usually very nice to me. In fact, the next time he saw me he apologized for his behavior and was back to his usual nice self." Amy explained. "How is Mr. Wold? He was such a nice man. I felt bad about refusing to talk to him, but Dr. Benton was so adamant about not talking to outsiders. Dr. Benton said my job was to answer the telephone and to refer people to the appropriate staff person."

"Mr. Wold is dead. He was murdered and that's the reason I am talking to you."

"Oh no! What happened? How did he die?"

"He was killed when his house blew up due to a gas leak. The killer almost got away with it, but our investigators found a gas pipe that was deliberately cut. Ken was my best friend and I remembered him talking to me about you and how you were initially very helpful."

"But, how am I involved in this?"

"My investigation of Ken's murder keeps going back to the suicide of a patient on his hospital unit. Ken had a hard time believing it was a suicide and he was doing his own investigation," John explained. "That was why he was talking to you. I believe he was killed because he was getting too close to the truth. Can you tell me everything you can remember telling Ken? You must have said something that was helpful to him. That's why he returned to talk to you for the second time. I know it has been a long time, but try not to leave anything out. Even the smallest thing could be crucial to my investigation."

"I guess it won't hurt anything now. I don't work for Albany Pharmaceuticals anymore. In fact, I'm mad at them for letting me go. Dr. Benton did tell me that it would be against the law for me to talk to anyone about my work without his approval, even after I was fired. Do you think I should get his approval before I talk to you?" Amy asked.

"I am sure he would not give you permission to talk to me," John said. "Dr. Benton may be part of my investigation. His name keeps coming up."

Suddenly, Amy looked at John with a startled look. "You don't think they let me go because I talked to Mr. Wold, do you?"

"Well, anything is possible at this point."

"Am I in danger?" asked Amy, in a fearful tone.

"No, I don't think so, especially since you talked to me. If anyone asks, just say you followed the rules and you did not say anything of importance to me. Tell them I asked questions about Ken and you really did not know him very well, which is the truth." John instructed.

"Now I'm starting to get mad. I was just trying to do the right thing. I did as I was instructed, and I still got fired."

"Go ahead and ask me your questions," Amy said. "I will try to remember everything I told Mr. Wold." John felt relieved. He thought he might have lost Amy and she would refuse to talk to him. He could understand how she might be afraid to talk to him, considering the circumstances.

"Is the name Dr. Rogers familiar to you?"

"Yes, he often left messages for Dr. Benton to call him. The number of calls from Dr. Rogers really picked up about six months ago. I remember him because he was often rude, and always seemed to be anxious and upset. The calls from Dr. Rogers suddenly stopped several weeks before I was fired. I also remember that Dr. Benton never asked me to call Dr. Rogers for him. He must have used a cell phone."

"How about the name Chad Turnquist. Is that name familiar?"

"Yes, and I remember telling Mr. Wold that Dr. Benson talked to someone with a name like that almost every week. I never saw the man; but I remember the name."

"You have been very helpful. I may be calling you in the future, as I accumulate more evidence."

"I'm glad you called, and not because I got a free lunch. I feel bad about Mr. Wold, and I do want to help find his killer, but I can't believe it was connected to Albany Pharmaceuticals. A lot of my friends work there, and the company has done a lot of good things for Milwaukee."

"Just one more thing. Can you think of anything that happened at the company while you were working there that was strange or different, anything at all?"

Amy was silent for a few minutes, trying to remember everything that happened during her short employment. " There was one thing that was strange and was talked about a lot at the coffee breaks. One of our scientists suddenly disappeared. His name was Dr. Sorenson and the girls decided that he must have been fired or moved on to another job."

"It was strange because no one knew anything about his departure. One day he was here, and the next day he was gone. Usually, there is talk about the next job people take, or the reason they are leaving. For example, they had a party for me when I left and everyone, including me, thought that I was let go for business reasons, not my work. After I left, there were several changes in the secretarial pool."

"What did the scientist look like?"

"I only saw him a couple of times. He was average looking, with dark hair. Oh! Now I remember, one of his eyes blinked a lot, like he had something in it."

"Was he heavy looking?" John asked, starting to get very interested after Amy mentioned Dr. Sorenson's blinking.

"He was not fat or anything like that. He may have been a little overweight."

"Is there anything else you can remember about Dr. Sorenson, even the smallest thing?"

"No, not really. The few times I saw him he was usually with another scientist who was really good looking, like you. That's why I remember them. The other girls and I talked about how nice it would be to date the good looking guy."

"Do you remember the name of the other scientist?"

"Yes," Amy said smiling. "It was Dr. David Bird."

"Thank you again, Amy. You have been very helpful. If you remember anything else, please do not hesitate to call me at this number." John handed Amy his card. "Remember, if anyone asks, you were not able to help me and we did not discuss Dr. Sorenson or Dr. Bird. I asked you about Ken and Chad Turnquist, but you were not familiar with the name Turnquist," John explained.

"O.K. thanks for lunch."

John expected someone would be following him. He thought that was O.K. because it meant he was on to something. John remembered Ken thinking someone was following him and it was probably true, especially since Ken was murdered shortly after he told John about his suspicions. Ken told John what kind of car it was, but John could not remember the description. John felt bad that he had not paid closer attention to what Ken had said. Having Ken's journal would have made things so much easier.

Dugan was talking to Benton on the new drop phone. Dugan had been following John since his arrival in Milwaukee and reported everything to Benton. "Do you want me to take care of the girl or the cop?" Dugan asked.

"No," replied Dr. Benton. "We can't keep killing people. The heat will only get worse. We probably should not have killed that social worker."

Benton was starting to regret getting involved with Dugan. He was too eager to kill people. He wondered how many people Dugan had killed. But, he had to admit, Dugan's services had been very valuable at times. "Keep following the cop and report everything back to me," Benton said.

Chapter Twenty-seven

John wanted to talk to Dr. Bird, but he thought he needed to put some heat on this Dr. Benton first. Things were starting to add up and Dr. Benton and Albany Pharmaceuticals were right in the middle of it. John admitted to himself that he liked to make the bad guys sweat. He also remembered Captain Arnold's warning to be careful about what he said to officials at the pharmaceutical company. If John pressed too hard, his superiors back home would hear about it and he would be asked to leave Milwaukee. He knew he was getting closer to the truth, and he couldn't mess things up now.

It took several phone calls before John could get an appointment with Dr. Benton. Finally, Dr. Benton agreed to meet with him. Dr. Benton met John at the receptionist's desk and escorted him to a small meeting room. Dr. Benton was also looking forward to the meeting because he needed to find out how much John knew. "What can I do for you?" asked Dr. Benton.

"I'm sorry to bother you, but I need to ask you a few questions. I am a detective with the Lawrence Minnesota Police Department. I am investigating a murder in Lawrence and I am in the process of tracking down leads," responded John.

"The leads must be very important for you to come all the way from Lawrence."

"Sometimes small leads turn into bigger ones," said John. "Several months ago you were contacted by a social worker from a hospital in Lawrence."

"Oh yes, I remember him. I'm not sure I was able to help him much."

"His name was Ken Wold and he wanted to talk to you about a patient you referred to a mental health unit in Lawrence."

"How is Mr. Wold?"

"That is one of the reasons I am here. Ken Wold was murdered and my investigation into his murder keeps coming back to Milwaukee and a patient you referred, Mr. Thomas Howell."

"I don't understand how the two are connected. Your own people investigated Mr. Howell's death and said it was a suicide."

John was getting tired of playing this game with Dr. Benton, but he continued on. "Ken came to Milwaukee to talk to you about Mr. Howell because he had questions about the suicide."

"I vaguely remember Mr. Howell. I believe we sent him to Lawrence because that facility had space for mentally ill patients that is hard to find, with all the changes going on."

"I understand you know Dr. Rogers."

"Oh yes. That was a factor too. Joe and I went to medical school together and I called him to see if he had room in his facility."

"I understand you treated Mr. Howell in the emergency room at Albany Hospital."

"I treat a lot of patients and, as you know, patient information is confidential unless you have a court order. In fact, I may have said too much already," responded Dr. Benton.

"So, you can't give me any information on Mr. Howell?"

"No, not without a court order. As I asked before, how are the two incidents connected?"

"They are not connected yet, but several things are beginning to point to a connection, and that is what I am trying to figure out now. One last question. Are you familiar with the name Chad Turnquist?"

"No, why do you ask?"

"His name and your name keep popping up in my investigation, and as I told you, I am following up on every possible lead."

Dr. Benton looked at his watch and said. "I have another appointment. Do you have any other questions?"

"Not right now."

"I'm sorry I could not give you more information. The confidentiality rules seem to be getting tighter all the time."

"I will try to have a court order the next time we meet. Thank you for meeting with me and for being so cooperative."

John was pleased with his meeting with Dr. Benton even though he did not get much new information. He expected Dr. Benton to hide behind the confidentiality rules. Dr. Benton was a smooth operator and handled all the questions well. All John wanted to do for the first interview was to plant a few seeds that might result in Dr. Benton becoming more concerned about his situation. He might even start to think about ways to protect himself. There were several contradictions between Dr. Benton's answers and other information John had accumulated, such as his relationship with Dr. Rogers. They were more than just former classmates. Now Dr. Benton would know that John was beginning to connect the suicide of Howell, the murder of Ken, and Chad Turnquist. What John could not figure out was what was behind all this violence. The two psychiatrists did not have a history of violence or any type of criminal activity. What was the motive? John asked himself. There is usually a reason for people's behavior. John's job was to find that reason.

Chapter Twenty-eight

It did not take John long to find Dr. David Bird. He was the only one in the telephone book. John knew this was a long shot, but he learned a long time ago that he needed to pay attention to even the smallest piece of information. The news that the missing scientist and the suicide victim both had a twitch or a tic in their eye aroused the interest of John and could or could not mean anything. But, it was enough for John to talk to Dr. Bird.

John knew he was being followed, and this was good, because it meant he was on to something. What that something was, he was not sure. John could easily lose the tail, but he was not sure he wanted to lose it. If the people following him found out about his talking to Dr. Bird, it might spook them into doing something drastic. But, since possibly two murders have already been committed, John did not want to put Dr. Bird in any danger.

John called Dr. Bird at his home in the evening. They agreed to meet at a small restaurant just outside of Milwaukee. John decided to lose the tail this time. That alone might get someone upset.

John had been deliberately vague over the telephone because he did not want to get Dr. Bird too concerned about the meeting. John quickly learned that he did not have to worry about Dr. Bird. Dr. David Bird was a young athletic looking person who looked like he could handle himself. John learned, in the small talk before the interview began, that Dr. Bird played tight end on the University of Wisconsin football team and had a black belt in the martial arts. John was looking forward to having Dr. Bird on his team.

Early in the interview, Dr. Bird revealed that he had very little respect for his supervisor, Dr. Benton. He indicated he had no intention of following Dr. Benton's order not to speak with anyone outside the organization. Dr. Bird knew he was a good scientist, had a good reputation in the scientific community, and could easily find a new job elsewhere. Dr. Bird was well aware of the millions of dollars he made for Albany Pharmaceuticals, and that the Board of Directors would think twice before they let him go, even if Dr. Benton recommended it.

John's primary problem now was how much information he should divulge to Dr. Bird. This was often a problem during an investigation. If you gave a person too much information, it might scare them off. If you withheld too much information, it could have an effect on the amount of crucial information a person might be able to provide voluntarily.

Dr. Bird impressed John as one of those people, like Ken Wold, who would start his own investigation, and John did not want that. John decided he would start slowly and divulge as little information as possible. Dr. Bird appeared to be a brilliant scientist and would probably start putting things together quickly.

"Dr. Bird, as I said over the telephone, I am investigating an incident in Lawrence Minnesota and one of the leads includes Albany Pharmaceuticals. Your name came up as a possible source of information, as being the friend of a missing scientist, Dr. Alan Sorenson. That is the purpose of this meeting, to learn more about Dr. Sorenson. You are not suspected of anything and you are not in any kind of trouble."

"I have to admit, I was starting to worry," said Dr. Bird. "It is not very often that a detective wants to question you. I was briefly reviewing my history to see if there was something I did wrong." They both laughed.

"What can you tell me about Dr. Sorenson?" asked John.

"We are friends, but not close friends. We are the type of friends who have coffee and lunch together, but not the type of friends who hang around together outside of work. Our interests and hobbies are quite different. Alan's primary interest outside of work is scuba diving. Every chance he gets he is off somewhere in the world diving. His enthusiasm about diving is so great that I have considered going with him. It just hasn't happened yet. Alan learned how to dive when he was a teenager and he usually spends his entire vacation diving in some exotic location. He says that floating on the bottom of the ocean, looking at coral and fish, is one of the greatest experiences of his life."

"Alan is very concerned about pollution of the ocean, the dying coral, and the excessive fishing. When he returns from a dive he writes letters to everyone he can think of, legislators, magazines, and pollution control agencies. He belongs to, and contributes to, all the environmental groups. The last time he came back from a dive he was livid. He changed airplanes several times and then took a boat to what was considered to be a very pristine part of the world, only to discover garbage floating in the water as he was getting ready to dive."

"Alan would raise hell with Albany Pharmaceuticals if he thought the company was involved in any type of pollution. I remember one time when the company had to stop operating in another country because of the havoc Alan caused. Alan did not care whose toes he was stepping on. If he were not a great scientist, he would have been fired a long time ago. The problem is, he makes a lot of money for the company with his research, and that is the most important factor to the Board of Directors. Albany Pharmaceuticals has brought to the market several excellent drugs that are very effective, and Alan and I have been major contributors to that success. I don't know for sure, but I would guess our contribution to the company is in the billions of dollars."

"What was the most recent project Dr. Sorenson was working on?" John asked.

"I'm trying to figure out why you are so interested in Alan," said Dr. Bird. "Has his recent behavior got him in trouble? Do you have him locked up somewhere? I can see Alan joining a group of radicals and trying to destroy something. He felt that strong about pollution."

"No, nothing like that. As I said, I'm just following up on names and situations that pop up during my investigation. Most of the time they don't amount to anything, but once in a while they lead to other more important questions. That is essentially my job, to try to put things together that make sense."

"About Alan's research. It is very complicated and it is even hard for me to understand at times, so bear with me. Alan's life, outside of the lab, revolves around scuba diving. The last few years he developed an interest in nitrogen narcosis which is a reversible alteration in consciousness that occurs while scuba diving at excessive depths. Alan even experienced mild symptoms while he was diving. All gases that can be breathed have a narcotic effect. As the diving depth increases, the effects of the gases may become more hazardous and the diver may become increasingly impaired. The depth at which narcosis will affect a diver varies widely from dive to dive and among individuals. Of course, there are some divers that like to push their limits."

Dr. Bird continued. "The most dangerous aspects of narcosis are the loss of decision making ability and focus, and impaired judgment and coordination. Other effects include vertigo and visual or auditory disturbances. Narcosis may cause extreme anxiety, depression, paranoia, overconfidence, and behavior that disregards normal safe diving practices. These are also symptoms that are experienced by many individuals who suffer from mental illness."

"Are you still with me?"

"Just barely."

"It doesn't get any easier. In his research, Alan is looking at neurotransmitter receptor protein mechanisms as a possible cause of narcosis. Proteins carry out most of the operations in brain cells. Proteins that are made in cells effect the functioning of the tissues that cells compose. Alan is following the theory that inert gases dissolving in the lipid bilayer of cell membranes causes narcosis. Or, put another way, oxygen flow to the brain, when interrupted, leads to disruptions in nerve networks."

"So," continued Dr. Bird. "Alan thinks that some mental illness symptoms might be able to be addressed through the manipulation of different gases. That is what he was working on when he disappeared. It sounds very theoretical, but that is the way Alan thinks. He is not very practical in his thinking, but his approach made a lot of money for the company, and that is the highest priority around here. They spend a lot of money on research and they expect high returns. The company will give you a few years to come up with a new medication that works, but if you don't produce, you are fired."

"Speaking of his disappearance, what are your thoughts about that?"

"It is not unusual for Alan to disappear for a few weeks." He would read about a new scuba diving experience in his diving literature and just take off. He would say something like " I'm off to the Red Sea for two weeks," and he would be gone. This time was different. He did not announce to anybody that I know that he was leaving and he has been gone for several months. He did not have any family that I am aware of and I am beginning to worry about him. He told me once about going to this great diving spot where the current was so strong that some divers were swept out to sea and never heard from again. He was becoming more and more adventuresome with his diving. I hope nothing bad has happened to him."

"What did the company think about Dr. Sorenson's research?"

"Well, it is interesting that you asked. Alan thought the company would be very supportive of his work because if he were right, it would change everything. The company response was very surprising to Alan and the rest of us. The company, or at least Dr. Benton, was very upset. I remember seeing Dr. Benton and Alan arguing, and Dr. Benton was livid. Now that I think about it, I think I understand the company response. Albany Pharmaceuticals has spent millions of dollars developing different medications for mental illness, resulting in billions of dollars in income to the company. Alan's research, if he was right, may have resulted in a different way to treat mental illness and much less income to the company. Most of us in the business realize that the current medications are probably temporary, and that there will be many changes in the treatment of mental illness as our knowledge of genetics and cell structure advances. In fact, there are several scientists currently doing research on aberrant proteins in nerve cells causing neurodegenerative disorders. I don't believe there is anyone, other than Alan, who is studying the effect of different gases on proteins. The company is very large and mental illness medication is just one part of our total sales, but if Alan was on to something, it would definitely hurt the stock and it would take several years to recover the losses," Dr. Bird explained.

There is the motive. John said to himself. Greed.

"Can you describe Dr. Sorenson in as much detail as possible. Maybe I can be of assistance in locating him."

"He was about five foot ten. Both of us are forty-two years old. His birthday was in August, two months before mine. Probably the most outstanding characteristic was a twitch in his right eye. He said he has had to live with it his whole life and that it made it difficult for him to attract women. He tried several times to have it fixed, but he was not successful."

"What color was his hair?"

"It was black, just starting to turn grey, like mine."

"Was he in good shape?"

"Yes, but he was just starting to get a role around his waist. I warned him about his eating habits, but he just laughed it off."

"Thank you for talking to me. You have been very helpful."

"You are welcome. Call me anytime, especially if you find out what happened to Alan. I still don't understand how he is involved in your investigation, but I'm sure you will tell me when it is the right time."

"You can bet on it," replied John.

Chapter Twenty-nine

"You were a detective at one time." John said to Captain Arnold when they met at the Milwaukee Police Department. "Do you remember the elation you felt when all the evidence finally came together and everything made sense, no matter how horrible and senseless the crime was?" This is the way I see it. Dr. Alan Sorenson, a brilliant scientist at Albany Pharmaceuticals, was working on a new, and possibly inexpensive way to treat mental illness. His supervisors at the company were afraid they would lose billions of dollars if he was correct. They managed to have him kidnapped and doped up. Under the name Thomas Howell, he was transported to the hospital in Lawrence and killed, making it look like a suicide. Ken Wold, the social worker at the hospital, had a hard time accepting the idea that Howell committed suicide. The more he looked into the suicide, the more he became convinced that it was murder. The killers decided Ken was getting too close to finding out the truth and had him killed. Sadly to say, the motive behind these senseless killings was money. Don't these people ever have enough?"

"I do remember experiencing the feelings you are talking about." Responded Captain Arnold. "But, I also remember the loneliness I felt, because I was the only one that understood the whole picture. I am not trying to depreciate what you are saying, because I have been in your situation. The problem is, the evidence you have is purely circumstantial and difficult to prove. Half the people in Milwaukee must have stock in Albany Pharmaceuticals. Are they all suspects? I am not going to arrest or even question somebody until I have more proof that they are guilty. What I will do is assign one of my detectives to look into this Chad Turnquist character. It sounds like he might be a hired killer and there might be other victims we have not heard of. The name is probably an alias, but we will check it out. You said you thought you were being followed. It would be helpful if you could get a license plate number," explained Captain Arnold.

"I tried to get a plate number but he never got close enough. Thank you for your assistance and support. I will come back with more evidence. I'm going back to Lawrence and go over all my notes to see if I have missed anything. I will also be talking to my supervisor and the county attorney. One thing I am sure of, I will be seeing you again."

Back in Lawrence, John was discussing the case with Lieutenant Shafer.

"It does make sense," said Shafer. "What is your next step?"

"I had better spend some time with my family before my wife asks for a divorce. She was stuck with taking the kids to all their different activities while I was gone."

"Take a few days off. I remember what it was like, getting so involved in a case that you forget everything else."

"Before I leave, I am going to ask our tech staff to see how much stock Dr. Roberts and Dr. Benton have in Albany Pharmaceuticals. I need to come up with some solid evidence that will impress Judge Seagram enough to open the suicide case."

"Knowing you, you will not drop the case mentally and you will be thinking about it all the time. Sometimes, a few days off helps to clear the mind and makes it easier to figure things out."

Just as Lieutenant Shafer said, during his time off, the case was all John could think about. He even had a hard time concentrating on his oldest son's baseball game. His wife almost kicked him out of the house as he sat around the house thinking about how he could get more solid evidence. The information on Albany Pharmaceuticals was on John's desk when he returned from his short vacation. Dr. Rogers had five million dollars invested in the company and Dr. Benton had nine million dollars worth of stock. It looked like they had recently switched all their stock holdings over to the company just before the stock price went up considerably. That sealed it in John's mind. It was all about greed.

John still needed to get more evidence to convict all the people responsible for the two murders. He wondered if there was anyone else involved, other than Rogers, Benton, and Turnquist. Currently, he had no reason to think there was anyone else.

John went to the county attorney's office to discuss the case and to develop a plan. The county attorney, Larry Ward, agreed with John, that he did not have enough hard evidence to proceed legally, but his reasoning made sense. "Rogers appears to be the weak link," said John. "He seems to get upset easily and hides it by acting angry and aggressive. It should not take much to scare him into confessing. But, if we can't break him and he tells Benton we are on to them, it will make it much harder to convict them. Benton will very likely get his high powered company attorneys involved."

"It appears to be worth a try," said Mr. Ward. "Just make sure that everything you say and do is admissible in court." Mr. Ward had worked with John many times and he was confident John would make sure he handled the investigation and interviews right. Mr. Ward had great respect for John and his professionalism, but he had to admit that John's relationship with Ken Wold was a concern. "By the way, what happened to the body of the suicide patient?" asked Mr. Ward.

John looked surprised and answered. "You know, that is something I overlooked. How could I have missed that? I'm going to check that out right away. I'll bet my suspects were involved in some way with the body's disappearance."

John left the county attorney's office on a high, thinking that checking on what happened to the patient's body could lead to further evidence. He went down to the coroner's office to see what happened to Howell's body. The secretary showed him the paper work she had on the body. "Mr. Howell's body was picked up by the Wagner Funeral Home after it was released by the police department," she said.

"Who signed for it?"

"According to the release form, it was a Dr. Joseph Rogers," the secretary replied.

Rogers again! John said to himself.

The next stop was the funeral home. John asked about the body. "The body was cremated the day after it arrived," said the funeral home director.

"Doesn't the cremation have to be approved by the coroner?"

"No, just an M.D. Dr. Joseph Rogers signed the authorization for the cremation."

"Who picked up the ashes?"

"Dr. Rogers told me the ashes would be picked up by a relative. According to the records the relative's name was Gordon Howell."

"What did Gordon Howell look like?" asked John.

"I was not here at the time. I will ask my assistant, Henry." The two men walked into the assistant's office.

"Do you remember the man who picked up Mr. Howell's ashes?" asked the director.

"Yes, vaguely. He was a tall man with blond hair."

"Could you pick him out in a line up?" asked John.

"Yes, I think so. He had a good build, like he worked out a lot." Henry said.

John asked for a meeting with Lieutenant Shafer and Larry Ward. He presented the new information on the cremation of Mr. Howell and the disposition of his ashes. He briefly reviewed the entire case, hoping to get the approval to arrest Dr. Rogers. "You have done a great job gathering evidence. But, it is all circumstantial, and we might have a hard time convincing a jury," said the county attorney.

"What else can John do?" asked Shafer. "It seems to me that he has done as much as he can."

"Somebody has to break," said John. "And that person is Rogers. Benton is not likely to do so, and Turnquist, or whatever his name is, can't be found unless Rogers or Benton give us more information. I have no reason to believe that anyone else is involved, but there could be another accomplice we are not aware of."

"O.K., I'll go along with you," said the county attorney. "How do you plan to do this?"

"I want you or Lieutenant Shafer to be in the interview room with me in order to demonstrate to Rogers, and his attorney if he has one, that we really are sure of our case and that we mean business. I want to embarrass and scare him as much as possible during the arrest and the interview. His tough talk is superficial and he is really a weak person. I want to give him a little hope, or something to look forward to, by telling him we will go easy on him if he gives up Benton and Turnquist," said John.

"Sounds good to me," said the county attorney.

"Lets do it," said Lieutenant Shafer.

Chapter Thirty

John and two police officers walked into the mental health unit at Arrowhead Hospital and asked for Dr. Rogers. "He is in a staff meeting," said the receptionist.

"Please show me where that is," John asked.

"Oh, you can't go in there," she said.

"Yes we can," said John. "Here is the arrest warrant." John and the police officers walked into the meeting room. "Dr. Joseph Rogers, please stand up. We are arresting you for the murders of Dr. Alan Sorenson, and Ken Wold." John read him his rights as the officers put the handcuffs on.

"You can't do this. Where is your court order?"

"Right here," said John, showing him the warrant. They marched Dr. Rogers out of the building with the staff and patients looking on.

"I want to call my attorney," said Dr. Rogers.

"We will let you make your call as soon as we get to the police station," responded John.

The first call Dr. Rogers made was to Dr. Benton. "I have been arrested. As far as I can tell, they know everything. They know Howell's real name and they said I am responsible for Wold's murder. You have to get me an attorney."

"Take it easy. What we don't want is for you to panic. We don't know how much evidence they have, and what they do have must be circumstantial. I can't be involved in getting you an attorney, and we can't use the company attorneys or we will look even more guilty. You have to find your own attorney and try to limit your calls to me," said Dr. Benton.

"You got me into this. You better get me out. I had nothing to do with those murders. It was all you and Turnquist."

"You have to stay calm. It would look better if we were not seen as working together. I will stay on top of things and try to figure out how we can get out of this. Above all, don't panic and do or say something that will hang us all."

The next thing Dr. Rogers did was to call a well known defense attorney in Lawrence, Brian Hannah. Mr. Hannah was not able to get free until late in the afternoon and Dr. Rogers refused to speak to anyone until his attorney was present.

John and the county attorney walked into the interview room and sat down across from Dr. Rogers and Mr. Hannah. "I'm glad your attorney is here Dr. Rogers," said John. "You have a very important decision to make today and Mr. Hannah should be able to help you with that. In case you don't know him, this is the county attorney, Larry Ward. He is here to help me explain some of the options you have."

"Who do you think you are, arresting me in front of the staff, putting handcuffs on me, treating me as if I was a common criminal?" Dr. Rogers said. "When this is over, I'm going to sue you and the police department. I know the mayor personally, and he is going to hear about this."

"This is what we know Dr. Rogers," said John. "We will explain your options to you later. Mr. Howell, the dead patient, was really Dr. Alan Sorenson, a brilliant scientist with Albany Pharmaceuticals. Dr. Sorenson came up with a theory about how to treat some forms of mental illness and was just starting his research on the theory. If he was allowed to follow up on his theory and prove it to be correct, it would have cost Albany Pharmaceuticals a great deal of money, because the company made billions of dollars on the medications it had already developed. The stock would have dropped, costing you and Dr. Benton a lot of money. Over the past ten years, the two of you have moved all of your money into company stock and you have profited greatly from the stock going up every year."

John continued. "Dr. Benton tried to talk Dr. Sorenson out of continuing with his research, but Dr. Sorenson was more interested in helping people than he was in making money for the company. Dr. Benton decided to get rid of Dr. Sorenson by doping him up and sending him to your hospital. You agreed to take Dr. Sorenson and to keep him drugged, at least on a temporary basis. At some point, you decided to have Dr. Sorenson killed and to make it look like he hanged himself. With your help, Chad Turnquist was hired by the hospital as a temporary employee and just happened to be assigned to your unit when Mr. Howell, or Dr. Sorenson, arrived. Turnquist killed Dr. Sorenson, making it look like a suicide. Everything was looking good and you thought you were going to get away with the murder. The coroner and the police decided that Mr. Howell hung himself. You arranged to have the body picked up and cremated because no one else claimed the body. You also arranged for Turnquist to pick up the ashes."

"One thing you did not figure on was Ken Wold getting involved," John said. "The more Ken looked into the suicide, the more questions he had. He scared you and Dr. Benton so much that you had Turnquist kill him by blowing up his house. Ken kept a journal of his investigation in his office and I am certain we will find the journal in your house when we search it. I'm assuming Dr. Benton asked you to go through Ken's office to see if you could find anything that would help me in my investigation."

"Dr. Rogers, we are arresting you for the murders of Dr. Alan Sorenson and Ken Wold. You may not have committed the actual murders, but you were involved in providing assistance to Chad Turnquist, and in helping to cover up the murders. That makes you just as guilty. Now, Mr. Ward will explain the options I was talking about," John said.

John and the county attorney had met before they talked to Dr. Rogers to plan their strategy. They realized that they could lose if the case went to court. They decided they would make an offer to Rogers and his attorney that would be hard to turn down. If they could get Rogers to plead guilty and testify against Benton and Turnquist, it would solve a lot of problems. They expected that Rogers had contacted Benton and that Benton was getting prepared to be charged with the murders. He had probably already contacted his attorney.

"Dr. Rogers, I want you and Mr. Hannah to listen closely to what I am proposing," said Mr. Ward. "After I am finished, we will give you plenty of time to talk with Mr. Hannah and make a decision. If you choose not to plead guilty, and you are found to be guilty by a jury, we will ask the court to send you to prison for the rest of your life, with no chance of parole or early release. If you plead guilty, and agree to testify against Dr. Benton and Chad Turnquist, we will ask the court to sentence you to twenty years in prison. With good time off, you could be paroled in fifteen years. We understand that you did not commit the actual murders and that you may even have been against having them committed. We know Dr. Benton was the mastermind behind everything, and that Turnquist, or whatever his name is, actually committed the murders."

"Dr. Rogers," said John. "You need to understand very clearly that this is the best chance you are going to get, and is the last chance to save yourself from a life in prison. You are definitely going to serve time. Your decision right now is about how much time you will serve."

Mr. Hannah requested a meeting room without a mirror or any type of listening device. He told Rogers that, based on only what John told them, he had about a fifty-fifty chance of beating the charge. As far as he could tell, the case against Rogers was based entirely on circumstantial evidence. It was possible that a jury could find him not guilty.

Rogers had been feeling guilty ever since Benton first asked him to take on Sorenson as a patient. The murders of the two men were a complete surprise to him and he felt trapped when Benton insisted that he help cover up the murders. He was relieved when Sorenson's murder was declared a suicide and he thought they were off the hook. Ken Wold's getting involved messed everything up. "I think I will take the deal they are offering me," Rogers told Mr. Hannah. "I am guilty of what they said I did. At least I can sleep at night."

Mr. Hannah came out of the meeting room with Rogers and requested a meeting with John and the county attorney. "Is twenty years the best offer you can make?" he asked.

"What kind of time were you thinking about?" asked Mr. Ward.

"How about fifteen years and Rogers tells the complete truth and testifies against Benton and Turnquist," said Mr. Hannah.

"O.K.," said Mr. Ward. "For Rogers' involvement in two murders, it is a good bargain and you know it. He is lucky to get this offer and it is the best he is going to get. Is this acceptable to you Dr. Rogers?"

Dr. Rogers looked like a broken man. He was no longer the confident, arrogant man he pretended to be. "I am going to plead guilty and take your offer," he said. John had a hard time hiding his excitement. Rogers could just as easily have gone the other way, pleading not guilty and going for an extended jury trial.

Dr. Rogers looked at John. "Your description of the way things happened was pretty accurate. I had nothing to do with the murders before they occurred. Dr. Benton asked me to take Dr. Sorenson for a few days in order to give him time to work on a more permanent solution. He did not say anything about killing him. I liked Ken Wold and I was completely surprised to hear of his murder. It was like being caught in a spider web with no way out."

"What was behind Sorenson's kidnapping?" John asked.

"Money. Contrary to what I have been preaching all my life, both Dr. Benton and I had all of our money invested in Albany Pharmaceuticals. Several years ago he talked me into moving all my retirement funds into the company, and we made a lot of money. We doubled our money in five years."

"Was Dr. Sorenson that much of a threat?" Mr. Ward asked.

"It was just a theory, but Dr. Benton apparently thought it was a major threat. He was afraid the stock would dive if word got out that many of the psychiatric medications the company produced were no longer useful. According to Dr. Benton, Dr. Sorenson was a very stubborn person when it came to his work and he could not be talked out of following up on his theory. And, Dr. Sorenson had a history of being accurate. Apparently he was a brilliant man."

"Dr. Benton also asked me to use my influence to hire Chad Turnquist so he could keep an eye on Dr. Sorenson during his hospitalization. Luckily, or not so lucky as it turned out, we had an opening on the unit for a temporary nursing assistant. Of course, Chad Turnquist was not his real name and I honestly don't know what his real name is," explained Dr. Rogers. "I tried several times to find out what his name was, but Benton was reluctant to divulge it."

"I was as surprised as anyone to find out that Sorenson had committed suicide, but I suspected that Turnquist had something to do with it, and I was right," Dr. Rogers continued. "The morning after the apparent suicide I received a call from Benton, telling me that Turnquist had staged the suicide. Benton said Turnquist found out that Sorenson was cheeking his medication, acting like he was taking it, but spitting it out after the nurse left. Turnquist told Benton that Sorenson was quickly recovering and was beginning to act normal. I am not sure, but I believe

Benton approved the murder."

"Anyway, Benton told me I had to do everything I could to make the murder look like a suicide and to protect Turnquist who was going to disappear. I arranged to have the body cremated and Turnquist got rid of the ashes."

Dr. Rogers continued with his confession. "We thought everything was going to work out until Ken Wold started to ask questions. Benton told me to watch Wold closely and to report everything to him. I wanted to back out of the whole thing, but I realized I was in so deep that no matter what I did, I was looking at prison time, and there was still a good chance we would not get caught."

"The more Ken looked into the suicide, the more concerned we got that the truth might come out," Rogers continued. "Now I know you are not going to believe this, but I was not involved in the murder of either man. As I said, I liked Ken and respected him."

"Again, I was shocked to hear about his death. I suspected Turnquist was involved, but I was not sure until Benton called me and asked me to go through Ken's office to see if he left any notes about the first murder. That was when I found Ken's journal. I have it at home, hidden in my office. Benton was right about one thing. Ken had done a lot of work on the suicide, and he was getting close to putting everything together. He would have made a good detective. When I heard that Ken and you were close friends, I knew we were in trouble. I thought it would be only a matter of time before you discovered the truth. I did not know what to do, but there was always a slim chance you would not figure everything out."

"Here is a pen and pad," said Mr. Ward. "I want you to write down the whole thing and sign it. We are going after Benton and Turnquist. Do not try to contact Benton and warn him."

I already called Dr. Benton," said Dr. Rogers. "From the little I know about Turnquist, he does not seem to care who he kills, so watch out for him."

"You have no idea what Turnquist's real name is?" asked John.

"Not really. I do remember Benton making a mistake one time. He called Turnquist something else. It sounded like Duncan," said Dr. Rogers.

Chapter Thirty-one

John called Jackson Arnold, the precinct captain in Milwaukee, and explained everything to him. "Looks like you solved the case," Captain Arnold said. "As I told you, this is going to be very sensitive, so I am going to contact the chief of police and get his input."

"I'm flying out in two hours," said John. "I would sure like to be there when you pick up Benton and Turnquist."

Captain Arnold went to see the Chief of Police, Duane Erickson, to explain the new evidence. "You are sure the doctor in Lawrence admitted to his involvement in the two murders and named Dr. Benton?" asked the Chief.

"They are sending us all the information right now. We should have it within the hour," said Captain Arnold.

"Albany Pharmaceuticals has a contract with one of the best law firms in the country," Chief Erickson said. "I think I will talk to the CEO about the wisdom of using his law firm to defend Dr. Benton. Benton could be the only one in the company who is involved in this mess. I will call him right now and make an appointment as soon as possible. In the mean time you wait for Detective Davis to arrive. He deserves to be there when we arrest Dr. Benton. Try to find out all you can on this Turnquist character. He sounds like he is a professional who may have a history in the state. Hopefully, Benton will give us his real name."

Chief of Police Duane Erickson walked into the office of the CEO of Albany Pharmaceuticals, William Mattson. "Hello Bill," said Chief Erickson.

"Hello Duane," said Mr. Mattson. "What can I do for you? You asked for an emergency meeting so it must be important." The two men have been friends for many years, played golf together, and watched the other person make a steady rise in their respective professions.

Chief Erickson explained the situation to Mr. Mattson. "My staff will soon be here to arrest Dr. Benton. He probably knows we are coming because Dr. Rogers, one of the accomplices, called him as soon as they let him make a phone call. Rogers was apparently angry because Benton immediately tried to put space between them and refused to help him find a good attorney."

"Dr. Benton is an arrogant, egocentric jerk. He has been trying to get my job for several years, and he was close to getting it at the last Board meeting," said Mr. Mattson. "He made a lot of money for the company over the last few years and that is what counts the most in our business."

"What I wanted to talk to you about, besides warning you of Dr. Benton's arrest, is the use of your law firm to defend him," said Chief

Erickson. "You have some very good attorneys and they could tie the case up for years. Your company has a very good reputation in the state and the country, thanks primarily to you, and it might not look good for you to have your attorneys defend Benton in a murder case. The arrest and details of the two murders will very likely be in the news for a long time. In fact, I will probably have to make a statement to the news media within the next few hours."

"So, you are suggesting that I not allow my firm to defend Dr. Benton," said Mr. Mattson.

"Well, it was just a suggestion," replied Chief Erickson. In my presentation to the news media I plan to make the point that your company had nothing to do with the two murders and that Dr. Benton is the only employee who was involved."

"Let me think about it," said Mr. Mattson.

"Thanks for seeing me on such short notice"

"And, thank you for warning me about the arrest," replied Mr. Mattson.

Chapter Thirty-two

John liked this part of his job, apprehending criminals after you finally have accumulated enough evidence. He was relieved when Rogers confessed. They could have been tied up in court for years. Rogers' confession came almost too easy. John was expecting a long battle with Rogers, but he seemed to be expecting to get caught and gave up easily. Rogers was quick to point out that he had nothing to do with the murders, and John believed him. Now it was time to arrest Benton and locate Turnquist. John wanted to be present when that happened. Two senseless murders had been committed and he would never see his best friend again.

Captain Arnold warned John that he was only there to watch and that he was not to say anything or draw his gun when Benton and Turnquist were arrested. John reluctantly agreed. Arnold reminded John that Albany Pharmaceuticals was a major employer in Milwaukee, and that Benton may be the only high level person involved in the murders. He also told John that the chief of police met with the CEO of the company to warn him of the arrest.

John, Captain Arnold, and two officers walked into Albany Pharmaceuticals. Captain Arnold asked the receptionist for the directions to Dr. Benton's office. The receptionist said she would call Dr. Benton. Captain Arnold showed her a warrant and told her not to call or inform Dr. Benton that they were on their way to his office. They walked into Dr. Benton's outer office, past his assistant's desk, and opened the door to his office. Dr. Benton was meeting with two other men. He looked up, shocked at the sudden intrusion.

"What is the meaning of this? You have no right to barge into my office." He was read his rights, handcuffed, and led out of the office. John nodded his head as Dr. Benton walked by. When they walked by Dr. Benton's assistant, he told her to call the company attorney.

Dr. Benton was sitting in the interview room waiting for his attorney to show up. He had refused to talk to anyone until his attorney was present. He knew the company had one of the best law firms in the country and he was expecting them to easily get him out of this predicament. He was not aware that Dr. Rogers had confessed and still was under the impression that all the authorities had on him was circumstantial evidence.

John was wondering why Captain Arnold was acting so smug about waiting until Dr. Benton's attorney arrived. After sitting in the interview room for two hours, Dr. Benton started to wonder about his attorney. The company attorneys were usually very punctual when he had called them in the past. He assumed his assistant had made a mistake and asked Captain Arnold for permission to call his attorney.

Dr. Benton called the office of his company attorney and asked to speak to the partner in the company, Simon Zimmerman, who was his primary contact person for legal matters.

Mr. Zimmerman informed Dr. Benton that he had been instructed not to get involved in the case because it was a personal matter, not a company matter. Dr. Benton asked Mr. Zimmerman to find someone to take his case, but Mr. Zimmerman told him he could not help him in any way. Dr. Benton was furious. He knew the company CEO was behind the law firm's decision not to defend him and he vowed that Mattson would pay for it.

He also decided he would replace the law firm as soon as he became CEO. Benton's immediate problem was that the company law firm was the only one he was familiar with and he did not know who to call. He decided to wave his rights to have an attorney present and see what evidence they had. That would help determine his next step. He asked to see the City Attorney, a person he knew, and someone he had played golf with a few times.

John, Captain Arnold, and the City Attorney, Charles Broman, walked into the interview room. Mr. Broman told Benton that since the murders were committed in Minnesota, Detective Davis would explain the evidence they had.

"Dr. Benton, your rights have been explained to you and you have been given the opportunity to have your attorney present at the interview. You have elected not to have an attorney present. You may change your mind at any time. Is that your understanding?"

"Yes. I may not need an attorney. I strongly doubt that your evidence will hold up in court."

John proceeded to explain the entire case against Dr. Benton. He finished his presentation by saying that he had a signed confession by Dr. Rogers, naming Dr. Benton as the primary person behind the murders. John told Dr. Benton that he would be transferred to Minnesota, charged with first degree murder, and held in jail until the trial was over. He also told him that he would also be charged with the kidnapping of Dr. Sorenson in the Wisconsin court system. "Now Dr. Benton, there is something else we are concerned about. The real killer, who we know as Chad Turnquist, is very much aware that you are the only person who can identify him. When he sees the news tonight, or reads the paper tomorrow morning, my guess is that he will seriously consider coming after you before you can identify him," John continued. "If you identify him now, the police will arrest him immediately. Because you were the primary person behind the murders, we are not prepared to offer you any leniency for identifying Turnquist."

"Since this is a very important decision for you, we will leave you alone for awhile to think about what Detective Davis said and to consider your alternatives," said Mr. Broman. Dr. Benton did not show his feelings in the interview, but he was shocked and scared about what was said. All that he had worked for was gone. "Damn that Rogers! "he said to himself. "I should have known Rogers would cave in, he is so weak. He probably got a deal for admitting to his role and blaming me for everything. "Dr. Benton told himself that Detective Davis was right about Dugan. He was a psychopath and would not hesitate to kill anyone, including Benton. Actually, that was what he liked about Dugan, he would do anything Benton asked.

Dr. Benton was worried about Dugan. That was one of the first things he thought about when he was picked up by the police. And, as the detective said, Benton had to make a decision about Dugan soon. The problem was, he would be admitting to his role in the murders if he told them where to find Dugan. But, if he could make it look like the murders were Dugan's idea, and not his, he might be able to get a lighter sentence.

That was what he decided to do, give them Dugan's real name and location, saving Benton from possibly getting killed, and place the blame for the murders on Dugan.

Knowing Dugan, it was very likely he would not give himself up, and would probably get killed in a shootout. In that case, he could easily blame the murders on Dugan, and get a more lenient sentence.

Dr. Benton asked to meet with the three men again. He told them Turnquist's real name, James Dugan, and as much as he knew about his location, which was not much. Captain Arnold left the room immediately to get his men ready to look for Dugan. Just as John expected, Benton tried to make it look like he was completely innocent of the actual murders. The only thing he admitted to was the planning of the kidnapping of Sorenson. He said he had asked Dugan and Rogers to watch Sorenson until he came up with a plan for what to do with him. He said he never instructed Dugan to kill Sorenson. Benton went on to say that Ken Wold's murder was a complete surprise. He said his instructions to Dugan were to follow Ken so they could find ways to discourage his investigation. After Ken's death, Benton admitted that he instructed Rogers to go through Ken's office to see if he could find anything that would implicate them in his death. He also said that Dugan volunteered to get rid of some of the other people Ken and John had contacted, such as Amy, the fired receptionist, Dr. Bird, and even John. Benton warned John and Captain Arnold about confronting Dugan because he was extremely dangerous. Benton was actually hoping that Dugan would be killed by the SWAT team so he could not give his side of the story.

Captain Arnold ordered his SWAT team into action. He told them Dugan was a hired killer and to quietly get the neighbors away from their homes. As John and Captain Arnold were driving to apprehend Dugan,

Captain Arnold reminded John that he was an observer, and that he was not to get involved in taking Dugan down. John wanted to be in on the action, but he understood the reason for Arnold's warning. John just appreciated the opportunity to be there when Dugan was captured.

As the SWAT team was evacuating the neighborhood, Dugan became aware of the changes in the usual neighborhood noises. More dogs were barking, the birds were quiet, doors were slamming, and people were talking. He looked out the window to see what was going on. He saw people leaving their houses, police cars parked in the street, and police officers everywhere. At first, he thought about trying to escape, but he realized the house was probably surrounded. He had numerous guns and enough ammunition to last for days. He decided to go down fighting and take as many cops out as he could. When he first got involved in this business, he vowed he would never serve time in prison again. He had served two years in prison twenty years ago for assault. He knew Benton had identified him and he wished he could kill him, but he also knew he would never get out of the house. He was angry with himself for not hiring someone to kill Benton in case something like this happened, and for not setting up an explosion that would kill more cops when they entered the house. He had made the mistake of being too sure of himself. During the gun fight, two officers were wounded and Dugan died in the exchange of gunfire.

Before John returned to Minnesota, he contacted Amy and Dr. Bird to tell them what had happened and expressed his thanks for their help. He told them that they were very valuable in finding the people who murdered Dr. Sorenson and Ken Wold, and that without their help he could not have closed the case. When John got back to Minnesota he contacted Becky and Diane to explain what happened and thanked all the people who were helpful in solving the case. John made it a point to include Ken's boys in his children's activities and to be as helpful as he could to Diane. Rogers and Benton pled guilty to kidnapping and as being accessories to murder. They are presently serving time in prison.

dreams

BY: GLENN JOPLIN

Contents

Dreams

INTRODUCTION

Monday, March 10th, 1965. Among the eleven babies born at West Rockford Hospital on this date are three who will meet later in their lives under special circumstances. The parents of these babies will have special dreams and expectations for their children's future, as all parents do. And, as with all people, the futures of their children will be determined by both heredity and environmental factors. The three babies will inherit special genes that will differentiate them from the other eight babies. The genes will be a major determinant in their lives, effecting every aspect of their adult life.

Dreams
Chapter One

Susan's Story

Wanda was exhausted. She had been in labor almost twenty hours. The contractions had been so excruciatingly painful that she thought she was going to die. She was very relieved when they finally injected the painkiller and it took effect. It all seemed to be worth it when the doctor placed her baby girl on Wanda's stomach and the nurses wrapped it in warm towels. Then the doctor cut the cord and tied it, placing the baby in Wanda's arms.

Wanda watched her baby nurse. "I'm going to name you Susan" she said. "Susan was my best friend in elementary school and she seemed so happy all the time. I want you to be happy more than anything. That's my dream for you."

Happiness was not something Wanda had experienced very often in her twenty years. She was one of ten children. It seemed like her father had always hated her. Her mother had an affair with another man while her father was in the Army, and Wanda was born soon after her father's return from the war. She never seemed to be able to please him, and he blamed her for all his problems. No matter how hard she tried to avoid getting hit, he always found a reason. Her father also beat her mother, and there were times when Wanda felt so sorry for her mother that she would stand between them, knowing that her father would take his anger out on her.

Wanda left home on her sixteenth birthday. She quit school and moved in with her boyfriend, Jack, who had also dropped out of school. He worked at the car wash and she got a job as a waitress. For a few months life seemed to be pretty good, then her boyfriend started coming home drunk. The physical abuse started slowly, as it usually does, with a shove during an argument over who should do the housework. Wanda said they should share the housework because she was working full time. Jack said housework was a woman's job and he wasn't about to wash dishes, make the bed, or vacuum the floor. As they continued to argue over his drinking, housework, and financial matters, the abuse progressed to slapping her face, especially when Wanda was winning the argument.

Wanda had lived with abuse all her life. Her father beat her repeatedly, and she had seen her mother get hit on numerous occasions. Although she did not like to get hit, she looked at abuse as normal behavior in a relationship. She was not aware that there was another way to live. In order to minimize the abuse, Wanda seldom challenged Jack, and only talked to him about controversial matters when he was in a good mood. She was not aware that her behavior served to reinforce Jack's use of violence. He quickly learned that the way to get his way, and to shut Wanda up, was to threaten violence. The relationship lasted two years, until Jack found another woman he liked better.

When Jack told Wanda he had found someone else, she was ecstatic. She had tired of him long ago and was only staying with him because she was afraid of what he would do if she left him. She now had her freedom, and for the first time in her life, at the age of eighteen, was free of an abusive man.

Wanda had a hard time enjoying her independence. For several months prior to her breakup with Jack, she had become increasingly depressed. There were days when she could hardly get out of bed. She felt listless and had difficulty concentrating. She experienced strong feelings of worthlessness and even entertained thoughts of suicide. At first, Wanda attributed the depressive feelings to her deteriorating relationship with Jack, but the feelings of depression continued after the relationship ended. Wanda remembered that her mother often looked and acted depressed, but at the time, Wanda attributed it to her mother having so many children, and to the abuse by her father.

When she was not feeling depressed, Wanda took advantage of her freedom. She went to as many parties as she could. Wanda had developed into a good looking woman and she found it easy to pick up men. She slept with numerous men and discouraged the men who wanted to get serious. It was also at this time that Wanda discovered alcohol. Although it did not last, Wanda found that alcohol helped her depression. When she was high, Wanda forgot her problems, and had a good time. It was when she came down off her high that she felt severely depressed.

Wanda gravitated from parties to the bar scene. At first, Wanda only went to bars with other women, and an occasional date. She gradually became a regular at a bar called Mac's which was located two blocks from her apartment. She developed the habit of going to Mac's every day after work, and would stay there for hours, often eating dinner. Mac's became Wanda's primary recreation and helped her forget her problems. It was at Mac's that Wanda met Frank.

Frank was eight years older than Wanda and had been married twice. He looked like a football player and Wanda was immediately smitten with his rough good looks. Frank was a crew foreman on the railroad and his work crew was often gone for weeks at a time, repairing rail lines. When he was in town, Frank was a frequent visitor to Mac's bar. Frank was an alcoholic, and had a terrible temper, especially when he was drinking. He was known as a womanizer and hell raiser in every town along the tracks. Frank was also a batterer. Both of his wives and several of his girl friends had left him because of the severe beatings he had given them. Frank had been charged with fourteen offenses involving assaults, stalking, and flouting orders for protection, and had repeatedly refused to get treatment for his abusive behavior and chemical dependency. The longest sentence he had ever received was a few months in the workhouse. When he did appear before a sentencing judge he usually got a stayed jail sentence, probation, or an order to seek counseling.

Frank was very nice to Wanda at first. He took her to Branson and Las Vegas, and spent a lot of money on her. He treated her like a queen and was careful not to lose his temper, especially when she had one of her depression spells. Wanda fell in love with Frank, and moved in with him two months after they met.

The first time Wanda experienced Frank's anger was when she told him she thought she was pregnant. He knocked the lamp off the table and tipped over the sofa, demanding to know why she hadn't used protection. He said he already had three kids to take care of and he didn't want anymore. When she told him she loved him and wanted to have his child, he almost hit her. He pulled his arm back to strike and she cringed, ready for the blow. He turned around, and walked out of the house, cursing and slamming the door.

One quality Frank was proud of was his sense of responsibility. He took his job seriously, and seldom missed work. His work crew was always the most efficient, and his supervisor knew that the job would be done right if Frank was supervising the crew. His supervisor was aware of Frank's reputation, but he left him alone as long as he got the job done right and on time. Frank was also against abortion and felt an obligation toward his children. His ex-wives were so relieved to be rid of Frank that they did not pressure him for child support payments, but he made a point to see his children and to give their mothers a little money. It was this sense of responsibility that led Frank to ask Wanda to marry him. If she was going to have his child, Frank felt an obligation to make it legitimate. It didn't seem to matter to Frank that he did not love Wanda. He had initially asked her to move in with him so he could have regular sex, and she was good looking and had a nice body.

Wanda was both surprised and elated when Frank asked her to marry him. When he finally came back, after blowing up, she expected him to kick her out of the house. They got married the next week in Las Vegas. When Wanda told her mother about the pregnancy and the marriage, she just shook her head. Her mother had heard about Frank's reputation and she knew what was in store for Wanda. She wanted to help Wanda, but she did not know what to say. She had been unable to do anything about her own abusive relationship. How could she help someone else?

The first time Frank hit Wanda was when he came home from work and Wanda was still in bed. She had been feeling depressed and was experiencing morning sickness. Frank's supervisor had questioned his use of overtime on the last job assignment, and Frank had been furious all day. When he came home and saw the dirty dishes in the sink and no dinner on the table, he lost it. He stormed into the bedroom, pulled Wanda out of bed, and knocked her across the room with the back of his hand. He called her a lazy bitch and pushed her into the kitchen, telling her to make his dinner. He got a beer out of the refrigerator and sat down to watch television. Wanda felt guilty about not having the house clean and not having dinner ready and told herself that she deserved to get hit.

Wanda was beaten two other times before the baby was born. Her obstetrician noticed the purple raccoon eyes, but was hesitant to pry. After every beating, Frank would apologize and blame it on his bad temper. He brought her candy and flowers, and was overly solicitous for days after the beatings. Wanda forgave him each time, and found a reason to blame herself for each beating.

When her baby was due to be born, Frank was working and Wanda took a taxi to the hospital. Wanda looked around the hospital room, wondering where Frank was. She knew he wasn't happy about having another child, but he should have been present for the birth of their first child. Frank had recently been spending less time at home and more time at Mac's bar. Last month, while she was shopping at the local grocery store, Wanda overheard two women talking about Frank and another woman. When Wanda confronted Frank with this information he became very angry, saying that he might as well have an affair if she did not trust him.

Frank walked into the hospital room six hours after Susan was born, carrying flowers and smelling like alcohol. He apologized for not being there earlier, saying that he could not stand blood or hospitals, and that he wanted to make sure it was all over before he came to see them. Frank held Susan, and Wanda noticed that his hand was almost as big as the baby. Wanda was hoping that, now that Susan was born, Frank would stay home.

Frank did stay home, for a week, then he returned to the bars. Wanda decided that the only way she was going to see Frank was to go down to the bar herself. So, when Frank was home from work, and Wanda was not feeling depressed, they could often be found at Mac's. They decided a babysitter was too expensive, and usually brought Susan with them. Susan became a regular fixture at the bars her parents frequented and knew many of the patrons by their first names. Susan would often get gifts of money or candy from the patrons. When bar owners refused to let Susan stay in the bar, her parents would tell her to stay in the car. Some days, she would stay in the car for hours, with nothing to do.

The beatings continued, often in front of Susan. On one occasion, Wanda went to the emergency room with a fractured cheekbone and a broken nose. Wanda had learned long ago that silence was the safest course.

The one time she called the police, they refused to arrest Frank and offered to take her to the hospital. She paid for it when she returned home.

Wanda finally decided to leave Frank when he hit Susan. She did not want Susan to go through the same thing she had gone through when she was a child. Frank threatened to kill her if she left, but she left anyway, and got a restraining order, keeping Frank away from her and Susan.

Wanda continued to experience periods of depression and to medicate her depression with alcohol. She became dependent on alcohol and was drunk almost every day. She stopped taking care of the apartment and herself. At six years old, Susan became the mother, taking care of Wanda, fixing her food, and trying to keep the house picked up. When the authorities discovered what was going on, they removed Susan from the home and declared both of her parents unfit to take care of her. Susan was placed in temporary foster care until a long term placement could be found.

For the next twelve years, Susan lived in ten foster homes and two group homes. Several times, the social service department tried to reunite Susan with her mother or father, but it never worked out. Frank was still abusive, and neither his fourth or his fifth wife wanted Susan around. Wanda had been hospitalized several times for her depression and her chemical dependency. Every time Susan was placed with Wanda, Susan became the caretaker, staying home from school to take care of her mother. When Wanda became depressed and stayed in bed, Susan would prepare her food and take it to her. She would help Wanda take a bath, and wash her clothes. When Wanda was drinking, she would stay out late, and would often bring a man home to share her bed. Some of the men tried to sexually abuse Susan, but she and her mother always managed to get them out of the house.

Susan always wondered what it would be like to live in a normal home, with a happy family. She envied the children in the families on television. They had problems every week, but they always seem to work them out, and the parents stayed together.

Some of the foster homes Susan lived in were very nice, and she especially liked the Peterson's. She lived with the Peterson's for eleven months when she was ten years old, and Mrs. Peterson often talked about adopting her. When she came home from school, Mrs. Peterson always had something prepared for her to eat. They would sit and talk about what happened to each other that day. Mrs. Peterson was someone Susan could talk to and she would tell Mrs. Peterson some of her deepest feelings and dreams. Mrs. Peterson was the first person she told about her sad feelings that would not go away, about feeling tired and irritable for no reason at all. Susan tried to talk to her mother several times, but her mother seemed to have too many problems, and Susan did not want to burden her with more problems.

During the time she was with the Peterson's, Susan's grades improved and she started to like school. Susan's self image improved and her social worker noticed that she was smiling more. Being a shy child, it took Susan a long time to establish friendships, but she found several girls in the neighborhood who would accept her and with whom she could have fun.

When Susan was almost eleven, everything fell apart. Mrs. Peterson became ill with breast cancer, and Susan had to be moved to another home. Susan wanted to stay with the Peterson's and take care of her foster mother, but the social worker did not think it was a good idea.

The shortest and most traumatic foster placement was one week at the Harrison's. Initially, Susan thought it was going to be a good place to live. She was thirteen years old, starting a new school, and she had her own room. Larry, sixteen, the Harrison's youngest son, and the only child still at home, had a room next to Susan on the first floor. The Harrison's had moved their bedroom to the basement in order to make room for Susan. They planned to use the money they received for keeping Susan to fix up the basement.

Susan was a pretty girl with long blonde hair and blue eyes. Her body was starting to develop and she was very self conscious about her breasts. She tried to hide her body by wearing oversize clothing. Susan's sad feelings were also increasing. Other people, with whom she came into contact, usually interpreted her sadness as part of her shy personality. She never lived in any one area long enough for people to get to know her, and she changed social workers so often that they were unable to recognize that Susan was a very sad person. She was also starting to experience strong feelings of anxiety for no apparent reason. There were times when she would sit for hours, wringing her hands and worrying about very minor things.

Larry had noticed Susan's maturing body and had difficulty keeping his eyes off her at dinner the first evening she was at the Harrison's. Susan was friendly with him because she wanted to make a good impression on his parents. Unknown to Larry's parents or the county social worker, Larry had a history of forcing sex on young girls in the neighborhood. Three of the girls were approximately Susan's age when he forced them to have sex. They were afraid of him because he had threatened to harm them if they told anyone, and to make sure they understood he meant what he was saying, Larry slapped each one and took a knife and acted like he was going to cut their breast. The sexual abuse had gone on for several years, and Larry became more daring and bold with each conquest. He started to think that he would never get caught and that he could do anything he wanted with girls. Larry saw Susan as easy prey. He told himself that, as a foster child who had lived in many homes, Susan had probably had sex with lots of boys. He was looking forward to years of fun with Susan.

The first night Susan stayed with the Harrisons, after his parents went to bed, Larry came into her room while she was asleep. He put one hand over her mouth, to keep her from screaming, and put his other hand on her breast. Susan tried to scream, but she could not make a sound because he had his hand tightly over her mouth. He squeezed her nipple hard to make it hurt, and whispered in her ear," If you make a sound I will kill you, do you understand?" Susan shook her head yes, and was starting to cry from the intense pain he was creating by squeezing her breast. Larry slowly took his hand away and released the pressure on her breast, ready to resume both if she tried to get away or yell. He raped her several times that night, and although it was painful each time, Susan found she could partially take her mind off what was happening by thinking this was happening to someone else, and not her.

When he was finally finished, Larry threatened to harm Susan if she told anyone. The next day, Susan stayed in her room, saying she was sick. She could not concentrate or make a decision on what to do. She sat, wringing her hands much of the day. Unknown to Larry or Susan, the rape had precipitated another episode of depression and anxiety, and Susan was literally incapacitated.

Larry was initially afraid that Susan would tell his parents. This was actually a key part of each rape, the intense anxiety he experienced after a rape, not knowing what the victim was going to do. It was a real high for him, almost as high as the power he felt before, during, and after a rape.

Susan's silence, similar to the other girls, was a signal to Larry that she really liked being raped. He had read somewhere, in one of the pornography books he kept hidden in his closet, that women really enjoyed being raped, and even dreamed about it sometimes. He couldn't wait until the next night.

Susan had lost her appetite and refused the food brought to her room by Mrs. Harrison. Her body seemed to ache all over and she could not concentrate. She asked herself what she could have done to encourage Larry to think he could have sex with her. People don't walk into other people's rooms and assault them. She must have done something wrong. Her negative thinking just reinforced the already low opinion she had of herself. For the first time in her life Susan started to think about death and suicide as a way out of her situation. All she could look forward to was a life of sadness and abuse. Life did not seem to be worth the misery she had already experienced in her thirteen years. She told herself that nobody cared for her and that no one would miss her if she died.

The following night Larry came into Susan's room and raped her again. This time, Susan did not resist and just lay there until he was finished. She did not have the strength or the energy to do anything. Of course, Larry interpreted her silence and lack of resistance as approval, and raped her every night for the next five nights. Each time, it was easier for Susan to remove herself from the event , as if she was a distant observer. After each rape Susan would take a shower, and rub her skin until it was red, trying to wash away the smell of Larry.

As Susan's depression started to lift, she thought more about what she could do to stop Larry. Apparently, he was not going to stop. The previous night, Susan had asked him not to rape her, telling him that she did not enjoy it and that it hurt. Larry just laughed at her, telling her that she wanted it as much as he did. He said that he read in a book that when women say no, they really mean yes.

Mrs. Harrison, oblivious to what was happening, tried to be nice to Susan. She thought Susan was sick, and the social worker had said that Susan was a very shy girl. When Susan asked to wash her sheets, Mrs. Harrison noticed the blood, but did not say anything, assuming Susan was having her period. Mrs. Harrison made a variety of food and bakery goods, trying to find what Susan liked to eat. She wanted to make sure Susan liked it at her house because they needed the money the county paid them to take care of her.

Susan was terrified of Larry, but she could not let the abuse continue. The social worker was on vacation and was not scheduled to visit the Harrison home for another week. Susan finally decided to tell Mrs. Harrison. When Susan told Mrs. Harrison that Larry raped her, Mrs. Harrison became very angry. "And when did he do this?" Mrs. Harrison asked. "Every night since I arrived," responded Susan, crying. Mrs. Harrison slapped Susan and said, "How can he rape you every night? "You must have encouraged him, you slut." "I knew I should not have asked for a girl." "I just thought girls would be easier to take care of." Mrs. Harrison said her son would never do anything like that and called Susan a liar and a whore. Mrs. Harrison told Susan to pack her things, and drove her down to the social service office.

The social worker on call took Susan to the emergency ward to have her checked out. The doctor said there were bruises, but he could not find anything else. The county attorney said he was not sure they could get a conviction because it would be her word against the Harrison's. The social worker said she would remove the Harrison's from the foster home list. At the least, Susan had saved other foster children from abuse by coming forward. Susan was placed in a temporary foster home until a more permanent placement could be found.

It was soon after the rape that Susan began to cut on herself. At first, it was accidental, when she cut her right arm with a broken piece of glass. The wind had blown the back door shut at a foster home where Susan was staying, and the window in the door had broken. As she was cleaning up the glass, a piece slipped and cut her lower arm. She watched the blood slowly flow out of the cut and seemed to experience a great relief. Her foster mother found her holding her arm and watching the blood flow. The foster mother quickly rapped a towel around the wound and told Susan to hold the towel while she drove to the emergency room. The wound was cleansed and needed ten stitches.

Susan could not get the accident out of her mind. For several days she was free of anxiety and all she could think about was the blood flowing out of her arm. A week later, Susan was shaving her legs in the bathtub and thought about the cut. She took the razor blade out of the razor and made a little cut on her left arm. Seeing her own blood seemed to relieve some of her bad feelings. She did not want to upset her foster mother again, so she put a bandage on her arm and wore a long sleeve shirt to hide the bandage. For several months, Susan was able to conceal her cutting by wearing long sleeved clothing. She alternated her arms and cut in different places so the cuts would have time to heal. The deeper she cut, the better she felt, and the harder it was to stop the bleeding with a bandage. It became increasingly more difficult for Susan to hide her cutting from others.

Susan was asked to leave several foster homes because of the cutting. The foster parents could not tolerate the cutting, blood on the towels and floor, and having to take Susan to the emergency room to close the wound. Susan knew it was wrong, but she could not stop. It was like an addiction. She thought about cutting all the time, and when she did cut, all her problems went away with the blood. Later, after her arm was stitched, she felt guilty about cutting and told herself and her foster parents that she would not do it again. But, the pressure would build up, she would become more anxious, and she would cut again. To Susan, the cutting seemed to be the only thing in her life that she had control over. Everything else in her life seemed to be controlled by other people.

Susan was placed in a group home when there were no more foster homes that would take her. In many ways, she liked the group home setting better than foster homes. The staff were usually young people in their twenties, and they worked in shifts. She seemed to be able to get along with them better than she did with foster parents, and there were several staff members she could talk with, and who seemed to understand her. Susan also liked being with other girls who had problems and past living situations similar to her own. There was even another girl, Diane, who had cuts on her arm. At the age of sixteen, Susan finally found a group of people with whom she could identify. Susan and Diane quickly became best friends and were always together. They shared their most intimate feelings, and when one would get depressed the other one would be there to help her.

Diane had been sexually abused by her father between the ages of six and twelve and was placed in a foster home after the abuse was discovered. Her little sister was almost six and Diane had become concerned that her father would start to abuse her. At the time she did not know what to do. If she told someone, it would break up the family. If she did not say anything, her father would continue to abuse her and would probably abuse her little sister. Her father said it was a special secret, just between them, and if she told anyone, it would destroy the family. When she finally told her mother, her mother got angry at Diane and called her a liar. When Diane realized her mother was not going to do anything about the abuse, she told her teacher. Her teacher told social services and there was an investigation. Diane's father acted shocked that she would accuse him of abuse and vehemently denied it to the authorities. The social worker said someone would have to leave the home, and Diane's mother said it should be Diane, much to her surprise.

Diane was now four years older, and like Susan, she had lived in several foster homes before being placed in the group home. Diane was certain that her father was abusing her sister, but she could not get anyone to believe it. When the authorities did question Diane's sister, she denied any abuse. Diane said, "Of course she would say that, look at what happened to me when I told the truth."

Diane and Susan would sit for hours telling each other what they would like to do to the people who abused them. Susan read in the paper that Larry finally got caught, at the age of eighteen, after breaking into a neighbors house and trying to rape their daughter. Several of his other victims, including Susan, came forth and testified at his trial. He had raped at least seven other girls, and not one had told anyone until he was apprehended and they knew he could not harm them.

Diane had started cutting on her arm a year ago. She too experienced great relief when she watched the blood flow out of the cut. One night, the two girls were talking about cutting and decided to do it together. Neither of the girls had cut for several months, and the staff thought that their being together was helping them to keep from cutting. When one of the evening staff was doing rounds, checking on everyone, she opened the door to Susan's room and saw the two girls sitting on the floor, entranced by the blood oozing out of their wounds. Other staff were called, and the girls were rushed to the emergency room. Both girls were well known to the emergency room staff and the procedure had become almost routine. "Well" the doctor said, " This is new, two at a time. Were you girls having a party?"

The next day, a meeting was called to discuss the cutting incident. Some of the staff argued that the girls should be separated and placed in different homes. They said the cutting would just get worse if the girls remained together. Other staff argued that the girls were good for each other and that the cutting was an isolated incident. Susan's social worker decided the county would be remiss in it's responsibility if the girls were allowed to remain in the same house. The girls pleaded not to be separated, but it was decided to move Susan to another group home.

Now what am I going to do?, Susan asked herself as she sat watching the T.V. She paid very little attention to the program that was on, but it did help to take her mind off herself at times. At age nineteen, Susan finally graduated from high school. Neither of her parents attended her graduation ceremony. Her father sent a card and twenty dollars. Her mother just sent a card. Susan could not be angry with either of them. Her father was living with a woman with five children and was unemployed. He had been fired from his job at the railroad after he hit his supervisor. He spent all his time at the bars and was a pathetic alcoholic. Susan's mother was currently in the state hospital for depression. She had been in and out of treatment facilities for chemical dependency and depression since Susan was first placed in a foster home.

It was decision time for Susan. The social worker was pressing her to make a decision about her future. Now that she had graduated from high school and was nineteen years old, she had to move out of the group home. The social worker encouraged her to go to vocational school or college, but Susan was tired of going to school. She worked part time at a local fast food restaurant her senior year of high school and liked the work. The manager offered her full time employment and she was thinking of taking it, even though it was at minimum wage and there were no benefits. The social worker tried to get her to look around for a job that paid more and had benefits, but Susan was comfortable working at the restaurant and was afraid to ask people for a job.

Susan and her social worker tried to work out a budget based on a minimum wage salary, and it just made her more depressed to find out there would be no money left over for recreation once they deducted rent, utilities, and food. She could not get sick because there would be no money available for the doctor or medication. Susan felt like curling up in her bed and forgetting the whole thing. There were just too many hard decisions to make. Up until now, Susan had not been expected to make decisions. The county always decided where she should live and where she went to school. Housing and food was free, and Susan received a monthly allowance for clothing and recreation.

After considerable hand wringing and encouragement from her social worker, Susan decided to share an apartment with another girl from the group home, Linda. Linda had moved out of the group home several months ago and was a very sociable person. The social worker thought Linda would be good for Susan and would help her to be more sociable. Linda was concerned about Susan's shy personality, but she needed to find someone to share the cost of the apartment.

Shortly after Susan moved into the apartment, Linda introduced her to the credit card. Susan was complaining about not being able to buy a coat she wanted and Linda said, "Use a credit card. I have three, and I can get anything I want." "You only have to pay ten dollars a month on each card." "You know that junk mail you always throw away? I'll bet you get a credit card application every week. Just fill one out and they will send you a card right away." Susan looked in the garbage can and found an application. She filled it out and mailed it the next day. As soon as she got the card, Susan went to the mall and purchased two hundred dollars worth of clothes. She couldn't believe how easy it was. She soon reached her maximum on the card and complained to Linda that she could no longer use the card. "Just apply for another card." Linda said. "That's why I have three." Soon, Susan had four credit cards, and was close to the maximum on each card. "This living independently wasn't so bad after all, she told her social worker, who asked to see the bills from the credit card companies. The social worker added the bills and discovered that, in six months, Susan had acquired a debt of five thousand dollars at an average interest rate of fifteen percent. The social worker tried to explain to Susan that she now owed the credit card companies not only the five thousand dollars, but an additional seven hundred and fifty dollars in interest a year. She told Susan that just to keep the interest paid up, Susan would have to pay the credit card companies almost sixty five dollars a month. The social worker told Susan to cut up her credit cards and that she would find someone to give Susan some advice on how to handle her debt.

Susan was devastated. She had screwed up her life again and couldn't seem to do anything right. The debt was like a big weight she could not get rid of and she sat for hours wringing her hands, telling herself she could never pay it back. She felt hopeless, and could not see one positive thing in her life. No one cared about her. She had a dead end job. Susan ruminated about her life for days, and the more she thought about it, the more depressed she became. She decided there was nothing to live for and decided to kill herself. Susan hated any kind of pain and knew she could not shoot herself or jump off a bridge. She remembered a girl at one of the group homes who committed suicide by taking an overdose of her medication. Susan decided to check Linda's room and see if she had any pills. She found some medication Linda's doctor had prescribed to help her sleep and thought that would be a good painless way to die. She swallowed the remaining pills in the bottle and laid down on Linda's bed to go to sleep for ever. Linda came home an hour later, called 911, and Susan was rushed to the hospital. Her stomach was pumped, producing pill fragments, and she was given activated charcoal, and admitted to the intensive care unit. She was moved to the psychiatric unit after she was stabilized.

"I can't even kill myself," Susan told Dr. Williams. "I can't do anything right." "Why do you want to commit suicide?" asked Dr. Williams. "You would too," responded Susan, "if you were in my situation. My parents are alcoholics and neither of them ever cared for me. If I did die, no one would come to my funeral. I've been depressed all my life. I don't care about anything or anybody. I haven't had a good nights sleep for years. I was raped when I was thirteen years old and no one would believe me, until the ass hole got caught for raping other children. I've lived in foster homes and group homes since I was six years old."

"Are all those cuts from suicide attempts?" asked Dr. Williams. Susan was wearing a short sleeved T-shirt. Her arms were full of scars where she had cut herself. "No, I just cut myself when I am feeling anxious. It seems to take away some of the bad feelings, to watch the blood flow out, and to see the open wound. It doesn't last long though. As soon as the wound is healed, I feel like cutting again. Sometimes I don't even wait for a wound to heal before I cut in a different place. I may have to find a new place to cut because my arms are almost filled up. "Susan continued, "This girl I met in the hospital cuts on her legs. Maybe I should start cutting on my legs."

"Why do I get depressed all the time?" Asked Susan. "At the present time you have what we call a double depression," responded Dr. Williams. "Apparently, you have been experiencing simple depression, which we call dysthymia, much of your life. It is a chronic, milder depression which lasts for years. Another form of depression is what we call major depression. Some of the symptoms of a major depression are listlessness, guilt, and inability to feel even a little better. "A double depression," continued Dr. Williams, "is when a person with dysthymia experiences a major depression, and that is what I believe is happening to you.

"Oh hell," said Susan, "Do you mean I have to put up with this all my life?" "I don't know," responded Dr. Williams. "What we can do is offer you medication that will make you less depressed, and hopefully make you feel better about life."

"I knew someone that said she got fat when she took medication." Susan said. "Yes," responded Dr. Williams, "there are side effects such as weight gain, hand tremors, dry mouth, and blurred vision." "Do you have a place to go when you leave here?" asked Dr. Williams. "Back to my apartment, I guess," responded Susan. "I don't want you to be on your own when you leave the hospital," said Dr. Williams. "You will still need some help." "I'll get Mr. Andrews, the social worker, to talk to you. He will work with your county social worker and try to find an appropriate place for you to live." "Not another group home," moaned Susan. "Maybe there is another alternative," replied Dr. Williams.

Chapter Two

Jason's Story

Sally Henderson looked around the hospital room. What a family! she thought to herself. Present were, her husband, Wayne; his brother, Ray; Janet, Ray's wife; Sally's parents, and Wayne's parents. The occasion was the birth of the first son in both families, Jason Wayne Henderson. As usual, every one was talking at the same time. Ray brought champagne and plastic glasses. It was only a matter of time before the nurse would ask them all to leave. Sally looked down at her son who was sleeping in the crook of her arm. "I'm sorry son, but you haven't got a choice. You are going to be an athlete. No matter what kind of dreams I might have for you, your father and uncle will make sure you play sports."

Jason's grandfather had been a good athlete and his father and uncle seemed to be involved in some type of sport all the time. If they were not playing, they would be watching a game on television. Wayne was an excellent baseball player in high school, and had a chance to make it as a professional, before he injured his knee in a slide, ending his dreams of being a pro.

Wayne and Ray had gone into the hardware business with their father and the family successes in sports helped the family business. Everyone knew the Hendersons and many of their friends stopped by the store to talk sports and buy something.

It was a good life, and the family couldn't wait until the next generation started to play sports. Jason had an older sister, Sonja, and his cousins were all girls. Wayne and Ray were beginning to worry that there would not be a boy to carry on the Henderson tradition. Ray's wife could not have any more children and that left it up to Wayne and Sally. It was a great relief to everyone when Jason arrived.

Wayne and Sally were married soon after they finished high school. He was the high school sports hero, and she was the beautiful cheer leader that cheered him on at every game. They had been going together for two years and everyone expected them to get married. At the time, Wayne was looking forward to signing with a professional baseball team and their future would depend on how well he did in the minor leagues. Everything changed when Wayne injured his knee. He was despondent for several months, but finally pulled out of it and went to work with his brother and father. Sally became pregnant the following year, and Sonja was born. Two years later, Jason came along.

For his first birthday, Jason received a toy football from his uncle Ray and a small glove and ball from his father. All the family was present except Sally's sister, Emily. Aunt Emily was five years older than Sally and she seldom attended family events. There always seemed to be tension in the house when Emily was present. She had a knack of getting into trouble, no matter where she was. She had never married and seemed to have trouble holding on to jobs. Her parents had repeatedly bailed her out of financial difficulties and the family often argued about how much help they should provide. Several family members had suggested she get professional help, but she always resisted. She was currently working for a restaurant chain somewhere in Florida.

Emily considered herself the "black sheep" of the family. When she was ten years old, she was sexually abused by her uncle and told the school counselor. Her uncle was convicted and sent to prison. She felt guilty about what happened to her uncle and thought her family blamed her for the abuse. When she was a senior in high school, Emily became pregnant and had a son. She was living with her parents and starting to get her life together when her son died of Infant Death Syndrome. Emily blamed herself for her son's death and thought the family felt the same way.

Emily had tried to go to college several times, but dropped out each time after a few months. Sometimes she would feel so depressed she could not get out of bed. Other times, she felt so good she would stay up all night. She would call people long distance, and talk for hours, running up large telephone bills. She would exercise for hours and seemed to have unlimited energy. She would get in her car and drive, with no destination in mind. There was no way she was going to see a doctor again. They were all quacks who tried to get people to take drugs. The one time she did go to a psychiatrist when she was feeling depressed, he put her on some type of medication. She got very sick and felt like a zombie.

The best thing for Emily and her family, she thought, was to be as far away from each other as possible. She missed her family, especially her sister Sally, but she thought this was best for everyone. She would have loved to have been there when Jason was born, and for his first birthday party, but she could not tolerate every one staring at her and asking her questions. It is no one's business how she is doing and what she is doing!

Jason was an exceptional athlete from the beginning. Wayne and Ray had been playing catch with him since he could walk. They took him to ball games before he was old enough to play and went over the various positions, explaining what each person did. Jason was not only athletic, he was also intelligent. He was a quick learner and seldom made the same mistake twice after he started playing. Wayne and Ray attended every game in which Jason played, and often, one or the other of them was his coach. Of course, since Jason was usually the best player, he was the pitcher on the baseball team, quarterback on the football team, and point guard on the basketball team.

Sally tried to get Jason involved in other activities, but she always seemed to be competing with Wayne and Ray. When she wanted to take him to the library, Wayne wanted to take him to a ball game or practice some sport with him. When Sally tried to get Jason to practice his trumpet or do his homework, Ray would come over and want to watch a ball game on television with Jason, pointing out the strengths and weaknesses of each player, as they watched the game.

Wayne and Sally often argued about Jason's future. Sally was worried that Jason would be a one dimensional person when he grew up. What would happen if he should be injured, like Wayne? What did Jason have to fall back on if he did not have sports? Wayne said Jason had great potential, and that he had to practice as much as possible if he was going to get a college scholarship. As long as Jason maintained a B average, he could get into any college, and that was all Wayne was concerned about.

The elementary and high school years went as expected. Jason moved from one sport to another, always the star. The other boys looked up to him, and all the girls wanted to go out with him. Wayne and Ray followed his sports career closely and were always willing to give him advice. Wayne was very proud that Jason was following in his footsteps. In fact, Jason broke many of the high school records set by Wayne.

Wayne and Ray would sit for hours, drinking beer and discussing Jason's future. Which sport should Jason select for college? Which college would be the best to showcase Jason's talents? What college coach would get the most out of Jason and realize his potential? Which professional sport would be the most appropriate, considering Jason's height, weight, and specific talents? To make it as a professional athlete, the planning has to begin as early as possible, and a person can't make too many mistakes!

Jason felt like he was on top of the world. He had just graduated from high school. He had received a full scholarship to play football at the University, and his girlfriend was the best looking and most popular girl in school. Wayne and Ray did not agree with his choice of sports. They wanted him to play baseball. Jason received scholarship offers in three sports. He selected football because he enjoyed the quarterback role the most, having the team depend on him, the glamour of the position, and the girls who always seem to be attracted to the quarterback. Playing professional sports was his goal too, and he thought he had the best chance of making it to the professional ranks as a quarterback. He was too short and a little slow for basketball, at six feet- two inches, and two hundred and ten pounds. Baseball players usually spend several years after college in the minor leagues before they get to the major leagues. And, nobody goes to college baseball games. Jason was in a hurry, he wanted to get to the pros as soon as possible so he could make the big money.

Although his grade point average was 3.0, Jason knew he was more intelligent than most people. He never really tried to get good grades. He just wanted to get by and get good enough grades to get into the college of his choice. Early in high school, Jason's mother, Sally, tried to get him to study and use his intelligence, but she gave up after his sophomore year. Sally received very little support from Wayne and the competition for Jason's time seemed to increase every year.

Sally diverted more and more of her time to Jason's sisters who were more receptive to her ideas. Sonja was two years older than Jason, and was the class valedictorian. She was now at the University, majoring in pre-med and getting and 3.8 grade point average. Tammy, the baby of the family, was a freshman in high school. She already knew what she was going to be, a successful businesswoman who made a lot of money and who could buy all the clothes she wanted. Her mother was a loan officer in the bank, and Sally often talked about the successful businessmen and how they became successful. Both of his sisters loved Jason, and they got along well, except for the usual sibling arguments. They were proud of Jason's accomplishments in sports and liked the attention they received of being his sister.

Jason's thoughts drifted to his girlfriend, Angela. They had been going together for a year now. Angela was also going to the University in the Fall, and they had had even talked about living together, and possibly getting married in a few years. They had been having sex for three months, and one time Angela thought she was pregnant. It was hard to stop and put a rubber on, but Angela was getting more and more insistent about using protection. She said she was too young to have a baby and she was not going to have an abortion.

Although he liked Angela a lot, Jason was not sure he loved her. He often thought about all the new girls he would meet in college and how tied down he would feel if he was going with Angela exclusively. He decided to wait until they started college before he broke up with her.

"Jason, the guests are starting to arrive, can you come down now?"

Even though Jason was not interested in using his intellectual abilities, Sally was very proud of the young man he had become. She had attended most of his games from the beginning, and she had even started to learn some of the finer points of sports, like what a slider does, the function of a tight end, and the difference between a power forward and a shooting forward. She would have preferred that Jason select a sport other than football. Football players get hurt a lot, and the higher a person goes in football, the bigger and tougher the opposing players get.

Sally liked Angela and her family. They belonged to the same church and they often sat together at ball games. Sally expected Jason and Angela to get married. She just hoped they would wait until they finished college. That was one of her regrets, that she and Wayne were married soon after they completed high school and that neither she nor Wayne had a chance to go to college.

"Have Dad and Ray started drinking yet?" asked Jason. "Ray brought over a six pack and they are watching some sports event," responded Sally. Jason was starting to worry about his father and Ray. They seemed to be drinking more all the time. When they drink too much, they start to argue, usually about sports or the business. Ray wanted to expand the hardware store and offer more items for sale. Wayne and his father thought the business was doing fine and were reluctant to expand and increase the debt load.

It was one o'clock in the afternoon and Wayne and Ray had already finished the six pack. Ray has two Driving While Intoxicated charges on his record, and he still drives when he has had too much to drink. The judge ordered him to complete an outpatient chemical dependency program, but he still can not admit to himself or others that he has a problem.

Angela was having her graduation party the same day, so they agreed to see each other after the parties were over. All the relatives were coming for Jason's party, except Aunt Emily. She was still living in Florida, and seldom communicated with the family. No one knew what she was doing, and, to the relief of her parents, she had not asked for money for several years.

Jason opened all his presents and cards. He especially liked the card from Aunt Emily. It was a picture of a baseball player hitting a home run. Her note said, "Hit a home run for me too Jason. Sorry I can't be there. I'm down here in Florida trying to show these people how to double their profits, but no one will listen. Maybe I'll go to Disneyland and see if I can help them. Love, Aunt Emily."

No one was aware that Emily had experienced a series of hospitalizations the last ten years. She had refused to allow the hospital staff to contact her family. When she did communicate with her family, it was usually when she was stabilized on her medication. When she was manic, and experiencing psychotic symptoms, she completely avoided contact with her family. Emily's letters were usually upbeat and her family had no idea she was so mentally ill. Emily had experienced eight hospitalizations, lived with three different men, and her life was a shambles. She had blown hundreds of thousands of dollars on business ventures, fancy cars, and sharp clothes. She had filed for bankruptcy twice, and the only thing that kept her from getting into further financial difficulty was her inability to get a loan. Her parents had stopped loaning her money a long time ago.

For years the psychiatrists had tried to control Emily's illness with neuroleptics such as haldol and thorazine. The side effects were so terrible that Emily stopped taking her medication as soon as she left the hospital. Ten years after her illness surfaced, lithium was discovered to be a good substitute for the neuroleptics. Her psychiatrist had a hard time convincing Emily to try lithium, but once she did, she discovered that it leveled out her mood swings, and, most important of all, kept her out of mental hospitals. The only problem now was her tendency to stop the medication when she was feeling good, thinking she did not need it anymore. She also came to realize, that by manipulating the doses of lithium, she could experience the manic highs she liked so well. In some ways, it was difficult to give up the ability to stay up all night, to be the center of attraction at parties, to accomplish more work in two days than other people could accomplish in one week.

In a few weeks Jason would be starting college football practice. He was excited and scared. Except for summer camps, he had never been away from home. He was worried about competing in the classroom and on the football field. He had been told that he would probably be red shirted the first year because the team already had three good quarterbacks. He knew he had to work hard on the practice teams to impress the coaches for next year.

Jason was still dating Angela, but had been trying to cool the relationship during the summer. They had decided not to live together and Jason was trying to put some distance between he and Angela, without getting her upset. He wanted to be free to date other girls when he started college. Angela could not figure out what was going on. One minute Jason would be warm and giving, especially when sex was involved, and the next minute he would be cool and distant.

Jason was still trying to figure out what happened to himself last week. All summer, he had been working two jobs, lifting weights, and playing legion baseball. Suddenly, he lost interest in everything, called in sick, and stayed in bed. He did not even want to see Angela. He started to question his ability to compete in college, and for the first time in his life, he felt hopeless and unable to do anything about it. Jason never told anyone about his feelings and everyone thought he had the flu. Now, he was feeling great and was back to his old self. In fact, there were times when he entertained the thought of going straight to the pros, and skipping college. He knew he was good enough to make it. He just needed a chance to prove it. To his knowledge, no quarterback had ever gone from high school to the National Football League. He could be the first!!

Jason's strange behavior had not gone unnoticed by his parents. They were starting to worry about him. Lately, he seemed to be more temperamental, and less easy going. He seemed to be more uptight, and would respond in an angry manner at the slightest provocation. Maybe he was working too hard, they thought. Maybe he was anxious about going to college. Maybe he and Angela are not getting along. Jason's parents had tried to talk to him, but he brushed them off each time.

Sally remembered having a similar experience with her sister Emily.

Emily also had suddenly become impossible to deal with. No one could talk to her without her blowing up and complaining that everyone was picking on her. Emily accused Sally of talking about her behind her back, and this hurt Sally deeply, because Sally looked up to her big sister and wanted to be just like her.

It was with mixed feelings that Wayne and Sally saw their son off to college. He had never been away from home for any long period of time. Much of their recreation had consisted of watching Jason play ball. For the last few weeks though, there had been a lot of tension in the home. It was like walking on egg shells. It was hard to admit, but, they were relieved to have Jason out of the house.

Two months after college started, Angela and Jason were sitting in the student union having a coke and hamburger. "I'm thinking of quitting college," Jason said. Shocked, Angela responded "Why? Why would you throw all your dreams away? What would you do?" Jason responds, "I think I can go straight to the pros. I don't need college. I know I'm the best quarterback on the team and here I sit, red shirted for a year, with four more years to play. Besides, the coach wants me to switch to defense. I'm a quarterback, not a safety! I'm thinking about trying out for the Redskins. My dad knows one of the scouts and all I need is to be discovered." Angela noticed that Jason was talking very fast and that his appearance was disheveled. Jason always paid attention to his appearance and this was one thing she liked about him. Today, his hair was uncombed, he had not shaved, and his shirt was hanging out of his pants. "Have you talked to your parents? What will you do if you don't make it?" asked Angela.

Jason was getting irritated with Angela's questions. Even Angela has no faith in me, Jason thought. Who needs her, he said to himself, there are plenty of women around. I don't need college. I'll make millions as soon as they find out how good I am. "What about after the pros? or, What will you do if you get hurt?" asked Angela. "I can always be a coach or TV color man." responded Jason. "Forget it, I thought you would be supportive, but you are just like my parents. You don't have any faith in me. "Jason said, getting up to leave. "And, our date is off tonight, find someone else!" Jason said angrily.

Angela was both shocked and embarrassed. Jason raised his voice at the end of the discussion, and all the students around them were staring at her. She couldn't believe what she just heard. This was not Jason, it was someone else!

Jason and Angela did not see each other for several weeks. Finally, she broke down and called him on the telephone. Angela invited Jason to meet her at a local restaurant, hoping to revive the relationship. She thought she still loved Jason. She had excused his inappropriate behavior, telling herself that it was just temporary, and attributing it to his disappointment with football. Angela had heard rumors about

Jason's recent wild behavior, but could not believe it. They had known each other for over ten years, and Jason had never behaved this way. Jason agreed to see her because he felt a little guilty about dropping her.

Angela could not believe her eyes when Jason walked in the door of the restaurant. He had a cigarette hanging from his lips and looked even more disheveled than the last time she saw him. For the first time in her life, Angela felt embarrassed to be seen with Jason. "How are you" she asked. "I'm OK" he responded. Jason was glad he dropped her. He could see the disappointment in her eyes. "Do you want something to eat?" she asked. "No, I just had breakfast" Jason said. Reluctantly, Angela said "I was wondering if you wanted to do something together, like go to a movie." "No" responded Jason, " I'm pretty busy." Both of them could tell, it was all over between them. "Call me if you want to get together." Angela said. "OK" said Jason, getting up to leave, "Thanks for everything".

Since the previous meeting with Angela, Jason had changed dramatically. He had become a chain smoker, and was getting high every weekend. He was experimenting with drugs, and would take anything that was offered, but he liked marijuana the most. He wrecked the car his parents gave him after graduating from high school. Jason dated a different girl every week and usually picked the girls that would go to bed with him the first night. He hung around with the drug using crowd all the time.

Jason barely made it through the football season and almost got kicked off the team. He missed numerous practice sessions, and his athletic performance went steadily downhill. Jason's coach called his father and told him that he was very concerned about Jason and his attitude. None of the coaches were able to talk with Jason anymore without him getting mad and walking out. If it were not for the relationship between Jason's father and the coach, Jason would have been kicked off the team a long time ago.

After seeing and talking with Jason, his parents were very upset. "He must be taking drugs," Wayne said. "He used to take care of himself. He never smoked, never got drunk, at least that I know of, and never acted like this. You can't tell him anything!" "And, if you try to tell him something, he gets angry and says to get off his back. He is even thinking about quitting college!" "What is this nonsense about going straight to the pros? His coach says he couldn't even make the freshman team now!"

Tears were streaming down Sally's cheeks. She was sure something dreadful had happened to her son. Last week, Jason had screamed at his mother over the phone, angry at her for not sending him the exact amount of money he had requested. Jason told his mother that if he quits school, it would be her fault for ragging on him all the time. Jason was coming home for the Christmas holidays, and for the first time in her life, Sally was not looking forward to seeing her son.

Angela gave Jason a ride home from college. She drove off quickly after dropping him off at his house, not even staying long enough to greet his parents. He had been extremely inappropriate in the car and she vowed never to see him again. Numerous times during the three hour drive Jason had attempted to fondle her, putting his hand on her breast and between her legs. He asked her to stop and have sex with him for old times sake. He smelled terrible, and insisted on smoking the whole time. When it was evident that Angela was not interested, Jason berated her for having sex with him in the first place, calling her an easy lay, and telling her that she was not a good sexual partner, comparing her with other girls.

Jason's parents were shocked when they saw him. He had shaved his head and was wearing an old army coat that came down to his ankles. His clothes were dumped in a black plastic bag that he carried over his shoulder. He was smoking, and looked like he had not shaved for several days. He grunted to his parents as he walked by them and went straight to his room. He put on some loud hard rock music and closed the door.

For several days, Jason acted confused and his behavior was even more bizarre. He would come downstairs for dinner an hour after he had finished eating. He could not follow a conversation, and would continually go off on tangents, talking about things that were not related to the topic of conversation. He smoked continuously, and became upset when his mother asked him to smoke outside, telling her she was an unfit mother and that she always picked on him and favored his sisters. Jason became angry anytime he was asked about school or football. In an effort to keep them quiet, Jason told them the truth, that he lost his football scholarship and that he was on probation for failing all his classes. "I don't need college anyway. I can do anything I set my mind to. I can be a pro in any sport. I have had numerous offers from professional baseball, football, and basketball teams. When other colleges heard I had been kicked off the team, I had scholarship offers from all over the country."

Wayne and Ray could not believe what they were hearing. Here was a young man with all kinds of potential, and he was throwing it away. They both thought about what they could have done if they had Jason's opportunities. What happened? It must be drugs! What else would cause such a drastic change in a person?

After a family discussion, it was decided that Wayne and Ray would take Jason to a highly rated chemical dependency program. Even though Ray had not taken the outpatient program seriously, he had developed respect for the staff he met, and he thought they were sincere and knew what they were talking about. Ray was sure they could help Jason.

"Jason" Wayne said, "There is something seriously wrong with you. We don't know what it is and you refuse to talk about it. We think it is related to drugs and we want you to go to a treatment program." "There is nothing wrong with me." said Jason. "If you don't want me here, I'll leave." "I was going to live with a friend anyway." "No" Wayne said, "You have to go with us." Jason thought about running, but one look at his father and uncle told him they meant business. If he resisted, someone might get hurt, and it might be him.

Jason and his family were greeted at the door of the chemical dependency treatment center and taken to a small office. A woman introduced herself as the admissions counselor and asked what the problem was. After hearing a description of the problem from Wayne, she asked Jason what he thought. "Sure, I've used drugs in the past," said Jason, "But I have not used since I came home from college." "I am not a drug addict" Jason said.

"What we can offer you," said the counselor, "is a two week evaluation." "During the evaluation, blood and urine samples will be taken to see what kind of chemicals are still in your body. You will be involved in individual and group sessions, led by professionals, to see how you function in different situations. A detailed history will be obtained by talking with you and other significant people in your life, such as your parents. You will also be given a series of psychological tests. Since you are not committed by the court, you will be here on a voluntary basis, and can leave at any time." "After the evaluation is completed, we will be able to determine whether or not you are chemically dependent and what type of treatment would be appropriate."

"Will you stay here for the evaluation?" asked Wayne. "I guess so, anything to make you happy." responded Jason, sarcastically. "But, I swear, I'm not chemically dependent." All the paper work was completed, and Jason was shown to his room after a tour of the facility. He did not say goodbye to Wayne or Ray, and did not look back.

Wayne and Ray left the treatment center feeling good. They were finally going to get some help for Jason. They might even salvage his sports career. A lot of athletes had overcome their chemical problems and gone on to play in the pros.

Two weeks later, Wayne and Sally arrived at the treatment center to discuss the results of the evaluation. Jason and two other people walked into the room after Wayne and Sally were seated. The other people introduced themselves as the program director and the psychologist. Jason still had an angry look on his face, and sat slumped in the chair, with one leg over the arm of the chair. The program director started the discussion. "Jason admits to having used marijuana, cocaine, and LSD" I knew it, Wayne said to himself. "The blood and urine samples show traces of chemicals, but not enough to have an effect on his behavior at the present time. We believe Jason when he says he hasn't used since he left college." "I told you so," said Jason, defiantly. The psychologist continues the discussion, "The problem is, the behaviors you described on admission are still present and were very evident during the evaluation. Jason has an inflated sense of power and importance, a lot of energy, and sleeps very little. He talks loudly, laughs when others are not amused, and can be very belligerent and hostile at times. As we told Jason, we believe he has a mental illness and we think he should be referred to a psychiatrist for an assessment and for medication." "I'm not crazy, you guys are. I'm not going to see a shrink." said Jason.

Wayne and Sally sat there dumbfounded. They did not know what to say. My son mentally ill! Sally thought to herself. "This is not the first time we have encountered this type of problem," said the psychologist. "Chemical abuse is usually the first thing parents think about when their children are having problems like this, and the two problems often occur together. Jason admits to using a variety of chemicals, and he definitely has a problem with chemical abuse, but we do not think he is chemically dependent at this time. If Jason continues to abuse chemicals the way he has in the past, it is very likely that he will become dependent. With regard to chemicals, he might be able to profit from an outpatient program, if he is motivated to stop using drugs. At the present time, Jason does not believe he has any problems, and it is unlikely that he could profit from an outpatient program with his present attitude."

"We do not believe that Jason's current symptoms are related to drugs and alcohol," continued the psychologist. "We think we know what the mental illness diagnosis will be, but we would prefer that you hear that from a psychiatrist. I could refer you to a psychiatrist if you wish. And, if Jason will sign a release of information, we could send the psychiatrist a summary of our evaluation." "No way" said Jason.

"This is one of the problems we often face," said the program director. "Jason is an adult, and he has to approve of any type of treatment offered. If he does not want to see a psychiatrist, take medication, or participate in a treatment program, he does not have to." "For example," continued the program director, "To make Jason go to treatment, you would have to obtain a court order, called a commitment. You would have to prove to the judge that Jason is either a danger to himself or a danger to someone else. We often have to wait until a person hurts himself or others, or threatens to do so, before he can be treated."

"As soon as I get home I'm moving out!" said Jason. "I'm tired of this crap. I told you I wasn't hooked on drugs and you wouldn't believe me." Wayne and Sally were driving Jason back from the treatment center. Sally was thinking to herself, (Maybe it is a temporary thing and Jason will grow out of it. No one in our family has been mentally ill. Maybe he needs to be less dependent on us and to grow up.)

"Where will you go?" asked Wayne. "Who will you live with?" "I was talking to Jim Johnson the other day, and he said I could live with him." said Jason. "He works at the warehouse and said I could get a job loading trucks with him." Wayne did not know who Jim was, but he thought it might open Jason's eyes to see what it is like to try to support himself on a minimum wage.

Jason left the next day. He seemed to be feeling better, and was even cheerful, kissing his mother good-by. He was very talkative, saying everyone starts at the bottom and that it would only be a matter of time before he would have his own trucking business. Sally remembered hearing this type of talk before, from her sister Emily.

Three weeks later, Sally and Wayne received a telephone call from Jason. "I'm in the psych ward at West Rockford Hospital. The police threw me in here after I got kicked out of a restaurant. I'm going to sue the restaurant and the police. You have to get me out of here. I'm not crazy like these other loonies in here."

In fifteen minutes Sally and Wayne were at the hospital. After listening to Jason for a few minutes, they knew something was wrong with him. He could not follow a conversation, would not let them complete a sentence, and got angry at them every time they asked a question. He hit the table with his fist, stood up, and started yelling at them. "You always take the other side. Why don't you ever take my side? Just get me out of here. I can't stand it."

Sally and Wayne asked to talk to one of the staff members. Jason agreed to sign a release of information to allow them to talk to the staff, hoping that it would help him to get out of the hospital. Tom Jenson, the social worker assigned to Jason, asked them to come into his office. "I wanted to call you when Jason came in to the hospital, but he would not let me," Mr. Jenson said. "What happened?" Sally asked, "How did Jason end up here? What's wrong with him? Why is he acting this way?" "According to the police report," responded Mr. Jenson, "Jason walked into the Little Italy restaurant without a shirt. The hostess refused to seat him without a shirt and he exploded. He started yelling that they could not tell him what to do. He said he was an important person, with contacts in the White House, and that they had better seat him or they would pay for it. The police were called, and when they arrived, he told them to back off or they would get hurt. He said he was a black belt in Karate and that they had better not touch him. It took four policemen to handcuff him and get him into the police car. He proceeded to kick out the window of the police car. They had to secure his feet and his hands to get him to the hospital."

Mr. Jenson continued," After Jason got to the hospital he continued to be threatening, and it was difficult to follow his conversation. His thoughts seemed to be racing. He was sexually inappropriate to the nurses and had to be placed in restraints after he jumped over the admission desk when staff refused to give him a cigarette. He did not calm down until the doctor ordered emergency medication, and we gave him a shot to reduce the hyperactivity"

Sally and Wayne could not believe what they were hearing. It was like Mr. Jenson was talking about a stranger. How could Jason have done all those things? They knew he was having problems, but not this bad. "Can we see a doctor?" Wayne asked. "Yes, of course," Mr. Jenson responded, "but first I would like to ask you some questions. It is very helpful in the understanding of a patient to get a good history. I will arrange for you to talk to Dr. Williams after we are finished."

Mr. Jenson proceeded to question Sally and Wayne about Jason's history, beginning with infancy. He was interested in any possible developmental problems Jason might have experienced. Mr. Jenson asked if Jason had a history of suicide or aggression, if he was ever hospitalized before, if he had any previous legal problems. He asked about education, religion, family circumstances, friends, military status, and vocational experiences. "Does anyone else in the family have a mental illness?" Mr. Jenson asked. Initially, Sally and Wayne said no, but after Mr. Jenson asked about family members who exhibited strange behaviors or chemical dependency, they told him about Wayne's brother, Ray, and Sally's sister, Emily. "Do you think there is any connection?" Wayne asked.

"Genetics in mental illness is very well established," answered Mr. Jenson. "The illness that Jason has seems to run in families and we seem to be seeing more and more cases of the affective disorders. The increase might be due to the stress and strain of our lifestyles." "Here is Dr. Williams, he will be able to answer your questions."

Mr. Jenson introduced Dr. Williams to Sally and Wayne and left the room. "What's wrong with our son?" asked Sally. "We hesitate to give a name to Jason's illness when he is so young," responded Dr. Williams. "We usually like to have a six month history of symptoms before we make a diagnosis. All of the symptoms we have observed and heard about, regarding your son, suggest that he has an affective or mood disorder which we call manic-depressive. It is also known as a bipolar disorder, because it has two sides or poles to it. One pole is uncontrollable elation and the other pole is inconsolable misery. If you were to put both poles on a continuum, with one at each end, your son would be somewhere close to the manic side because he has more manic symptoms than depressive ones. In our language, we call that Bipolar I, as opposed to BipolarII, where a person has more depressive symptoms than manic symptoms"

"Manic symptoms," Dr. Williams continued, "almost always alternate with periods of depression. Some relatives or parents are so happy to see the manic symptoms depart that they do not realize a person has slipped into a depression." Sally then remembered the week last summer, when Jason stayed in bed almost all week and seemed to lose interest in everything. At the time she thought he was sick with the flu.

"How did he get this illness?" asked Wayne. "We don't know how it works yet," responded Dr. Williams, "but it appears that the bipolar disorder is transmitted genetically. It is not known whether it is caused by a single gene or by many genes acting together. The first episode of bipolar illness is often related to an emotional loss or crisis." "Genetic factors make a person more susceptible to mood disorders, but a trigger, such as a serious medical condition or psychological stress, is often what causes the disorder to emerge."

"How do you treat the illness?" asked Sally. "We use a combination of drugs and psychotherapy," answered Dr. Williams. "The illness is now much less distressing and destructive for the patients and their families than it once was."

"Why would a person stop taking a medication that works so well?" asked Wayne. "It happens far too often, "responded Dr. Williams. "Patients stop taking their medications for a variety of reasons. Some patients deny they have a mental illness and don't believe they need to take medication, like Jason is acting now. Other patients stop taking the medication after the symptoms are gone, believing that they don't need medication anymore. Still others stop taking medication because of the side effects."

"As I indicated," said Dr. Williams. "One of the difficulties in treatment is ensuring that the patient does not quit taking the medication. Patients often report that life on medication is dull compared to the energy and elation to which they have become accustomed. Patients need to continue taking what we call a maintenance dose, even when there are no symptoms."

"So, where do we go from here?" asked Sally.

"Your son," responded Dr. Williams, "needs to remain hospitalized until we can stabilize him on medication. If he is cooperative with taking the medication, and is not too intrusive or aggressive, we should be able to treat him here and he should be able to be released within a few weeks to one month. If he is uncooperative, we may have to commit him for a longer hospitalization. You can help us by talking to your son and getting his cooperation."

"No, I'm not going to stay here!" shouts Jason. "There is nothing wrong with me! I'm not mentally ill." "The doctor says they will commit you if you don't cooperate," said Sally. "What does he know, he's just a quack," responded Jason.

After stomping out of the meeting with his parents twice, and accusing them of conspiring against him, Jason finally agrees to take the medication and to stay at the hospital. "If I'm not out of here by the end of the month, I'm going to take off," Jason said. "And, I'm still going to sue the restaurant and the cops. They had no right to treat me the way they did. Get me a lawyer. Tell Mr. Spindler I want to see him as soon as possible. He will help me if you won't."

Sally and Wayne drove home, exhausted and devastated. The dreams they had for their son were gone. He would probably be mentally ill the rest of his life. What kind of life could he expect to have? If it was like the last six months, it was going to be tough for everyone. They talked it over and decided to get some books on the illness. If Jason was going to be sick for a long time, they would need to know how to work with him. Sally decided to call her sister, Emily. Maybe she could help them understand what Jason is going through.

Chapter Three

Debbie's Story

Joan looked down at her baby girl. She was so perfect in every way. She had her whole life ahead of her and she could be anything or do anything she wants. She and her husband, David, had agreed on a name several months ago. They would name their second daughter Deborah, after Joan's grandmother. As Joan lay in the hospital bed she wondered about the future of her new baby. "What kind of dreams or hopes do I have for you? Happiness would be number one I guess. Then, maybe good health and some kind of success. "

Joan enjoyed her life, but she always wondered what she could have accomplished if her life had been different. She and David had met in college and were married soon after they graduated. Marriage was important to her family and Joan had felt pressured to get married. It wasn't that she did not love David, she just wondered what she could have done or been if she had not married so soon. Mary, their four year old, came along almost nine months to the day after they got married, and all of a sudden, she had a family to care for. Joan had worked as a physical therapist during her pregnancy. She and David had talked about the importance of staying home with the baby, and she had passed up a promotion to stay home and take care of Mary. Joan had also wanted to return to college, get an advanced degree, and teach some day. She had not worked since Mary was born and she always felt like there was something missing in her life.

Joan's mother was a nurse supervisor and she always stressed hard work and responsibility. Joan had worked hard in school and was the class valedictorian. Her parents were very proud of her accomplishments, but Joan felt like she never could quite measure up to their expectations. Joan vowed she would never do that to her children. Sure, professional success was important, but there were more important things in life, like happiness and good health. But, Joan thought, happiness for one person may not be the same for another person. Is happiness achieving the goals you have for yourself, and how are those goals implanted in you in the first place? This is getting too complicated, Joan thought. How did I get on this stream of thought anyway? You were the cause of it baby, Joan said to herself, as she was looking at her sleeping child, so contented. I was day dreaming about your future, what life will be for you. Well, I hope you get a man as good as your father.

Joan looked over at David, sleeping in the chair. He had been up all night with her and fell asleep soon after the baby was born. They had gone to the hospital when she first started having labor pains. Mary was staying with the neighbors. The doctor sent them back home, saying it was too early, but the pains increased, resulting in their return to the hospital a few hours later. David held her hand as long as he could. The nurse asked him to leave and he seemed to be relieved, thinking he had done all he could to help his wife. Now it was up to the professionals.

David was a good husband and father. He didn't make a lot of money as an office manager, but it was steady work and he managed the family finances well. They had purchased a house two years ago and they were able to keep up the payments on the house and the car. Sure, it would have been easier to have Joan work, but they had agreed that she would stay home until all the children were in school. They were lucky to have good health insurance through the hospital where David worked. Almost all their medical bills were paid by the insurance.

David had been hoping for a boy. He loved Mary and he knew he would love the new baby, but there was something special about having a boy. In a way, it completed the family. Maybe next time, he thought to himself. David also had dreams for his children. He wanted his children to be successful and he worked hard with Mary to instill in her a love for books and reading. If he could get his children to love reading, they would do well in school and life. For him, reading had always been a way to relax, to experience adventure, to broaden a person's understanding of life and the world.

David believed there were two basic kinds of people, those who were closed, and those who were open. Closed people believed there was only one way to do things, one way to see things, one religion, one lifestyle, one way to treat others. Closed people see things in black and white, and think their way is the only way, the one true way, and refuse to consider alternatives.

Open people see things in greys. They believe there are many ways to look at an issue, depending on a person's life experiences. Open people ask how can people believe in one religion when there are so many, and each religion believes it is the one true religion. Open people are more accepting of differences and different opinions. Open people are willing to discuss an issue and consider another person's point of view. Open people are more likely to compromise and to consider all the alternatives before making a decision.

Of course, David saw himself as an open person. He saw himself as being more tolerant and accepting of others. The problem was, when you see grey all the time, you have trouble making decisions. Sometimes he envied closed people who have all the decisions made for them.

Debbie was a good baby. She was not fussy or colicky. She seemed to be a happy baby and smiled often. David and Joan had learned a lot from raising Mary, and they were much more comfortable and sure of themselves with the way they treated Debbie. She was loved by everyone, including Mary, and seemed to respond to the love in a very healthy way.

Two years after Debbie was born, Jeremy came along. David finally got his boy and both he and Joan decided that was enough children. Everyone was talking about the population explosion, and they even felt guilty about having three children.

Joan had been on birth control pills in between children, but they were worried about Joan taking the pill for the next twenty years, and the possible health problems. They experimented with other birth control measures and talked about Joan having her tubes tied. David read an article about vasectomy as a birth control measure and decided it would be the most appropriate and least traumatic type of permanent birth control. Joan was very appreciative of David's decision and was very solicitous when he came home from his vasectomy. He asked for a big bag of ice and went to bed with two martinis and the bag of ice between his legs. He quickly recovered and the decision appeared to be the right one. They could have sexual intercourse anytime and not have to worry about Joan becoming pregnant.

Debbie was not sure about her new brother. He got a lot of attention that she used to get. Even Mary played with him. Debbie's feelings of jealousy, coupled with her being in the terrible twos, made for a rough time for everyone in the family.

When Debbie was approximately six years old her parents noticed a slight difference in her behavior. She seemed to stay by herself more than Mary did at the same age. Even though she played with other children, she didn't have that closeness with another child that so many children develop.

Debbie was pleasant to be around, but there was something different about the way she acted. Other children noticed it too, and had a tendency to stay away from her or make fun of her. Some of the children were mean to her, especially the girls who formed clicks and who would turn their backs on her when she came near. David and Joan attributed her behavior to childhood differences. For the most part, they were not aware of the way she was treated by other children, because it usually occurred at school. They were not that concerned, as long as she seemed to be making progress in every other way.

Debbie loved to be alone. She could sit for hours and daydream. She would picture herself as the heroin in some of the stories her father read to her. He read to the children almost every evening, and Debbie looked forward to his reading so she could lose herself in his stories. It was easy for her to remember the stories and she could quickly lose herself in one of the stories, no matter where she was.

When Debbie was seven years old and in the second grade, her parents got a baby sitter and attended the elementary school open house. This was a chance for parents to visit with the teachers and discuss the progress of their children. Joan and David always looked forward to the open houses and the chance to talk with the teachers. There were the usual folders full of pictures and work the children had completed. Mary, of course, being the first child and very conscientious, always got glowing reports. The teachers could not say enough positive things about her. She was intelligent, cooperative, and very helpful. Most of the other children liked her, and the teachers had a hard time coming up with any type of suggestions for improvement. The teachers always said about Mary "If only the other children were as good as as Mary." Debbie was a different story.

Mrs. Anderson, Debbie's second grade teacher, was seated at her desk when Joan and David walked in. Mary had been in Mrs. Anderson's class four years ago and the Simpsons and Mrs. Anderson had met several times in the past.

Mrs. Anderson started the conversation by saying, "I don't want to alarm you, but Debbie seems to have a few problems. She is easily distractible and tends to daydream a lot. Often, when I ask her a question about the topic the class is working on, Debbie will act like she has not been paying attention." "She is smart and can recover very quickly," continued Mrs. Anderson, "but it is obvious that she is thinking about something else. She also has a tendency to isolate herself from the other children. During recess, I will often see her playing alone, as if she is in her own world. She usually gets along well with the other children, but she does not have a special friend like children often do at this age. Debbie does not appear to be as physically coordinated as the other children, and possibly because of this, she is reluctant to play games such as kick ball or dodge ball. She would prefer to sit and watch the other children play".

"Something happened the other day," Mrs. Anderson continued, "that also made me concerned about Debbie. Jenny Rooks, one of Debbie's friends, fell off the merry-go-round and started crying. Instead of helping and consoling her, like the other children, Debbie just walked away."

"On the more positive side, Debbie is one of the more intelligent children in class. She has better language development than most of the other children, and she gets her work done quickly. Her spelling and math work is very good, as you can see by all the good marks on her papers.'

David, trying to find a reason for Debbie's questionable behavior, asked, "Do you think Debbie might be bored in class?" "Maybe the work is not challenging enough for her." "We work with the children at home, and Debbie loves to have me read to her." "I have heard that intelligent children often get bored with school when the curriculum is not challenging for them." "I understand that you have to meet the needs of all the children in class, and the brighter children often get bored."

Mrs. Anderson, feeling a little defensive, said, "But Debbie is different. "I know what you mean, and I do try to offer the more intelligent children additional work. Mary was as intelligent as Debbie is, but she did not isolate herself as much as Debbie and she was not so easily distractible.

"Yes" countered David, feeling a little irritated by Mrs. Anderson's apparent defensiveness, "but Mary and Debbie are different children , with different personalities, and they should be expected to respond differently."

Joan, feeling the increasing tension, tried to be a mediator and cool things down. "We will try to pay more attention to Debbie, and hopefully she will grow out of some of the problem areas you have identified."

Mrs. Anderson, unable to let it drop, added, "Sometimes a child's problems in school are related to problems in the home." "Is everything all right at home?" This statement really got David upset. He just about said it was none of Mrs. Anderson's business. Joan grabbed him by the arm and said "No, there are no problems at home. Thank you for your time. I'm sure you have other parents to see."

Joan had to admit , she was concerned about Debbie. She and David had noticed Debbie's tendency to isolate herself when she was at home. It did not seem to be a big problem because they knew she could always be found in her room. And, she did respond when someone sought her out.

David and Joan discussed the meeting with Mrs. Anderson on the way home. David was still steamed at Mrs. Anderson for suggesting that there was something wrong at home. "The nerve of that woman. Who does she think she is? I think we should have Debbie transferred to another second grade teacher." "What good would that do?" responded Joan. "We thought Mrs. Anderson was a good teacher when she had Mary." "In a lot of ways she is right," said Joan. "Both of us have noticed Debbie acting somewhat peculiar. Maybe we are too close to her and too accustomed to her behavior to notice how different she is." "Well," said David, "Let's pay more attention to her and try to help her become less isolated and detached." "I will try to include her in more of the things I do, and try to do fun things with her." "And I will make it a point to talk to her every day after school and invite more children over to play with her," responded Joan.

The Simpsons devoted considerably more quality time to Debbie, sometimes at the expense of the other two children, but the characteristics described by Mrs. Anderson did not go away. At every teachers conference, the same complaints were repeated. Debbie was socially withdrawn, seemed to daydream a lot, was physically uncoordinated, and seemed to lack empathy. Her intelligence and ability to quickly comprehend classroom assignments kept her in the top ten percent of her class, and were able to dilute the negative characteristics. Debbie's teachers and parents began to accept the negative characteristics as part of her personality and stopped trying to change her. As long as she got good grades, and was not a trouble maker, no one became overly concerned. "She will grow out of it," they thought.

The other children in Debbie's class and neighborhood were also aware of her peculiar characteristics. Some of the boys called her names and made fun of her inability to play sports as well as the other children. When she did play, she was always the last one to be chosen to be on a team, and she would always be assigned to a position where she could do the least damage, such as right field. Debbie learned to hate sports because it was always connected with ridicule and failure. Mary was very protective of Debbie. Any child who made fun of Debbie had to answer to Mary and was likely to get a verbal thrashing and an occasional push. Debbie idolized her sister. Mary could do everything well and everyone liked her.

Mary knew Debbie was different, but she loved her brother and sister and she had been taking care of them since they were born. Mary had always been mature for her age and very responsible. When she was twelve years old, her parents started to let her do the baby sitting and she took her responsibility very seriously. She had become accustomed to Debbie's strange behavior and she had learned to just leave Debbie alone when she isolated herself. Debbie never caused trouble, and seemed to be very content to be left alone. Their favorite time was when Mary would read to her brother and sister, just like her parents did. They never seemed to tire of having someone read to them.

Debbie was twelve years old when her parents noticed that she seemed to be getting much more emotional. She was quick to anger and quick to cry. It seemed like every time someone tried to speak to Debbie when she was day dreaming, she would get angry at them. She also developed more physical complaints. Almost every week the school nurse would call, saying that Debbie was complaining about having stomach cramps or headaches. She also complained about sore muscles after physical education classes. It was at this time that Debbie started to menstruate. Both Joan and the school nurse assumed Debbie's increased emotional reactions and numerous physical complaints were due to the changes in her body. Joan remembered that she had a terrible time adjusting to her menstruation. The problem was, Debbie's intense emotional reactions seemed to be occurring more often and were not cyclical. Debbie also learned how to use her complaints to her advantage. If she was able to look real sick, she would be sent home from school and could stay in her room. For Debbie, this was the maximum reward, to be home, in her room, with no one to distract her. She could daydream all day.

Debbie started to get interested in boys when she was fifteen years old. Tom Harris was two years older than Debbie and had a nice car. He worked at the supermarket after school and on weekends. Debbie and Tom went to the same church and her parents liked Tom and his parents.

Tom's interest in Debbie increased as her body began to develop. Debbie was a pretty girl, with long dark brown hair and large brown eyes. Her skin was smooth and one of her teachers told her she could be a model some day. Although Debbie never took her good looks seriously, she did try to take care of herself and always looked nice.

It was about this time that the first real family crisis occurred. Mary, who was four years older than Debbie, had left home to attend the University. It was hard on everyone to have Mary gone. She had been such an integral part of the family. She was the only person Debbie could talk to, and her parents depended on her to help guide the younger children. She was so level headed and seemed so sure of herself.

Soon after Mary arrived at the University she fell in love with the star football player and was swept off her feet. In order to please her boyfriend, she started going to parties where alcohol, drugs, and sex was the primary recreation. Mary knew everything was going too fast, but she could not or would not stop.

It was the Winter break from college, and Mary was devastated. She was two months pregnant and her boyfriend had dumped her soon after learning she was pregnant. She could not stop crying and she and her mother had long talks about her options. Her mother told her that the family would support her no matter what decision she made, and the decision was her's to make. Joan tried very hard to present the pros and cons of Mary's options in a neutral manner.

Debbie was not included in much of the conversation, but she was able to gather enough information to know what was going on. Mary decided to get an abortion and to take a quarter off from school to recover from the emotional trauma. This was a good time for Debbie because she and Mary were able to have long talks together. Debbie vowed to herself that she would not have sexual intercourse until she was married.

Debbie and Tom had been going together for six months and he was starting to put pressure on her to have sex. They had been doing heavy petting for several months and it seemed to be getting harder to get him to stop. One night, after an especially heavy petting session, Tom blew up and said he could not stand it any longer. He gave Debbie an ultimatum, either they have sex or the relationship was over. Actually, Debbie had been close to giving in, but when Tom presented it as an ultimatum, she became angry and told him to take her home.

One week later, Debbie saw Tom kissing another girl. Debbie believed she was in love with Tom and that she could not live without him. All she could think about was having lost Tom for ever. She thought about calling him on the telephone and trying to get him to come back to her. When she finally got the nerve to call him, he hung up on her. When she tried to talk to him at school, he ignored her.

One night, Debbie's parents had gone to watch Jeremy play basketball, leaving Debbie at home alone. Debbie was often left at home, and she preferred it that way. Her parents knew Debbie had broken up with Tom, and they assumed it was a typical teenage romance from which Debbie would recover.

After seeing Tom with another girl that day, Debbie decided to kill herself. She had convinced herself that she could not live without Tom, and that she had lost him forever. Debbie went through her parent's medicine cabinet, took out all the pills, and put them in a cup. She put on her favorite music, and laid out on the chair the clothes she wanted to be buried in. She sat down at her desk and wrote her parents the following note.

Dear Mom and Dad,

> I feel so sad. There is no reason to keep
> on living. I am sorry that it had to be this
> way. I love you very much. Tell Mary and
> Jeremy that I love them too. If it is OK with
> you, I would like to be buried in the clothes
> on the chair. Good Bye.
>
> > Love,
> > Deb

Debbie sat down on the side of her bed and took the pills, a few at a time, with water to wash them down. She did not like to take pills and she gagged every time she tried to swallow a bunch. When she was finished taking the pills, she laid down on her bed to wait for death.

For some unknown reason, Joan was feeling very uncomfortable at the ball game. Debbie had kissed them both when they left for the game. Debbie had never been known for being affectionate and she had never kissed them before when they went out for the evening. She also had a strange smile on her face throughout dinner. Joan told David she was going to call home and check on Debbie. There was no answer and Joan became worried. She told David she was going to drive home and asked him to catch a ride with the neighbors.

When she got home, Joan went straight to Debbie's room. Debbie looked like she was asleep. Joan saw the empty pill containers, quickly read the note Debbie left, and called 911. Joan tried to wake Debbie up, but she would not respond. She felt her pulse and it was still beating. As soon as the ambulance arrived, Joan gathered all the pill containers and went with Debbie to the emergency ward. The emergency technicians in the ambulance called ahead with a description of the medications Debbie had swallowed. The staff at the emergency ward quickly pumped Debbie's stomach and gave her charcoal to counteract the medication. The doctor praised Joan for her quick thinking and for remembering to bring along the empty pill containers. Debbie stayed overnight at the hospital and returned home the next day.

Joan and David were upset, angry, embarrassed, and very concerned. How could Debbie do such a thing? How could they have missed the signals? If Joan had not come back early, Debbie might have died!! What have they done wrong?

Debbie was feeling very guilty for having put her parents through such an ordeal. As soon as she had taken the pills, she knew it was a mistake, but she thought it was too late, and had resigned herself to dying. Debbie could not understand why she was unable to look at alternatives. Now she could see all kinds of alternatives and suicide was not one of them. All she could think about at the time was the rejection by Tom and not being able to live without him. She could think of all kinds of reasons not to commit suicide, and Tom certainly was not worth it.

Joan and David had always tried to give their children the best of everything. They could not understand how this could happen to their family. They knew Debbie was different from other children, but they always expected her to grow out of the peculiar characteristics she exhibited. They attributed them to childhood and adolescent stages. The past year they had experienced two major crises, Mary's pregnancy and subsequent abortion, and now Debbie's suicide attempt. What next? Joan and David started to question and re-evaluate their parenting skills. What had they done wrong in the way they raised their children? Do they need to change something to keep Jeremy from experiencing a similar crisis? They even questioned the way the other spouse treated the children. Joan had always thought that David was a little too strict with the children. He made them eat all the food on their plates. On one occasion, Joan remembered, David made Debbie sit for an hour after dinner before she finally finished eating. He had also been very strict about their dating, wanting to meet every boy who came to the house to pick up the girls, embarrassing both the girls and their dates. One time, David got so angry with their messy rooms that he made the two younger children work all weekend cleaning the entire house.

David had always felt that Joan was too soft on the children. When the children were very young, they had discussed their differences in their approach, and had agreed not to try to over-ride the other parent's decision, no matter how wrong it appeared. They had agreed to talk with each other when they were away from the children if they disagreed with the decision of the other person. But, David thought, several times Joan had gone to the children's rooms after he had restricted them. Had she tried to undermine his authority? Every time a new fad came out, Joan would buy the children what they wanted.

Joan and David began to question every decision they made. Their confidence level went from high to very low in a short period of time. They even started to question their decisions outside of the family.

They became more tentative on their jobs and in their relationships with other people. David was always joking with people and saw that as an important characteristic in getting along with people. After Debbie's suicide attempt he stopped joking with others so much, and when he did try to make a joke he questioned the impact it might have on the other person each time, taking away the spontaneity. Joan asked herself if the problems were related to her returning to work. She had returned to work when Jeremy started the first grade. Even though she and David had agreed to her working outside the home, she felt guilty when the kids were left with a baby sitter or were home alone after school. Of course, Joan's mother-in-law had not helped matters, expressing shock that she was not going to be home when the kids came home from school. Her mother-in-law said that was one of the most important times for the children. Joan remembered the good times when the children returned from school. She always had a snack waiting for them and the girls talked about their experiences for the day. Some days it was hard to say anything because the girls wanted to talk so much. And the bad days, when one of the girls would come home crying and would pour her heart out about being called a name or not being included in a certain group of girls.

Joan had returned to the hospital as a physical therapist. The job was very rewarding, giving her a chance to get out of the house and to build her self esteem. She had not worked since Mary was born and she had questioned her ability to return to work. She found that it had not taken very long for her to regain her confidence on the job, thanks to a refresher course. Now she had lost confidence in her primary job, being a mother.

Yes, Joan thought, maybe I should have stayed home. Maybe the children would have been more stable and had fewer problems. At the time, Joan convinced herself that she would be a better mother by returning to work, and the children would grow emotionally by being more responsible and independent. Yes, she said to herself, it was always a hectic time, coming home from work, tired, having to cook dinner and meet the children's needs at the same time. And, there were the sick days. David had agreed to share some of the burden when one parent had to stay home from work, but the major part of the burden fell on Joan's shoulders. Her accumulated sick leave from work was always close to zero because of her need to stay home with the children when they were sick. She didn't even have time to get sick herself! And, her sick leave was always an issue at evaluation time. Her supervisor made a big deal of her low accumulation of sick leave and bragged about all the sick leave he had accumulated. One time she almost asked him how many times he had stayed home with the kids.

For several months after Debbie's suicide attempt, the Simpson household was very tense. Joan and David had agreed to take turns staying home with Debbie until she had recovered. They had decided to give Debbie her space and not to pressure her to talk about the suicide attempt, even though they both wanted to ask her "WHY." Debbie slowly opened up and told them both she was very sorry. She explained her feelings about Tom and feeling rejected. She did not want them to be mad at Tom so she did not tell them about his pressuring her to have sex.

Debbie returned to school two weeks after the suicide attempt. Her parents made an appointment with a psychiatrist at the local mental health center, but cancelled it after Debbie assured them that she was over Tom and that she had no plans to hurt herself. Of course, the other students heard about the suicide attempt, and it was the main topic of gossip for days. Now her classmates really looked at her as different, and most of them stayed away from her. Some of her classmates stayed away because they did not know what to say around her. Others stayed away because they did not want to be seen with a "weirdo." And there was the usual group who made fun of anyone who was different. Debbie wasn't bothered too much by the shunning because she had always been a loner, but she could not help thinking that others were talking about her behind her back.

There were a few students who tried to help Debbie. Caroline had gone to school with Debbie since the first grade. She was as close to Debbie as a person could be. Debbie would not let anyone get too close to her, but she and Caroline were good friends, and Caroline made it a point to show Debbie that she was there if she needed a friend now. Tom Harris knew why Debbie tried to commit suicide. Even though he thought it was stupid, he did feel a little guilty. He also tried to talk to Debbie and be friends with her, but she did not want anything to do with him.

Debbie settled back into the school routine and was able to catch up on the school work she had missed. She dated a few boys, but never allowed the relationships to get serious. Debbie was very wary about getting serious with another boy. It was too painful. Debbie's grades improved, and she worked hard at developing and maintaining friendships with both boys and girls. She was beginning to enjoy her high school years, and her relationship with her family improved considerably. The suicide attempt was forgotten, as Debbie seemed to be making progress in every area and was developing into a beautiful young woman.

The voices came on slowly. It was in September, just after Debbie started her senior year of high school. At first she thought the voices were coming from a radio or TV and ignored them. One night, on her way to a football game, Debbie realized the voices were coming from her head. A voice said, "You are a worthless bitch. You should die." Debbie had borrowed her mother's car and almost hit another car because she was so upset. She turned the car around, drove back home, went to her room, and put on her head phones, hoping to drown out the voices. She could not understand what was happening. The voices were so real, but how could they be in her head? What would her parents or friends think if she told them about the voices? They would think she was crazy. "I really am strange".

Debbie was frightened. She did not know what was happening to her. She tried to think back. " Was it something I drank or ate? People act strange when they are on drugs. Maybe someone slipped something in my food. She did not know who to turn to so she kept her fears to herself and isolated even more so from family and friends. She started walking around town alone and often would be seen by others talking to herself. She did not tell anyone about the voices for several months.

Debbie slowly arrived at the point where the voices were always with her. They were as much a part of her life as any part of her body. She responds to the voices, argues with them, and often does what they tell her to do. She tries to tell the voices she is not going to listen to them, but they just get stronger. She knows other people do not hear voices, but, it is the others who are different, not her. Debbie's feelings have changed lately also. She constantly feels anxious and tense, and can't seem to concentrate. Her mind wanders constantly in class and she can't sit still long enough to do her homework. She has difficulty going to sleep at night and often dozes off in class. She has completely withdrawn from the other students. When other students try to talk with her she gets upset and walks away.

Debbie's parents were shocked when she told them she had quit school and was going to move out of the house. Joan and David had been worried about Debbie's increasing isolation and they too had observed her talking to herself. It looked like she was arguing with someone else, but there was no one around. They often heard her in her room, talking loudly and angrily. On one occasion they heard a scream and quickly ran to Debbie's room, thinking she was injured, only to find her laying on her bed cuddled up in a fetal position, rocking back and forth.

Several times the Simpsons tried to get Debbie to see a doctor. They talked with the family physician who said it could be a number of things, including drugs. He said he would run a series of tests if they could get her into his office. Debbie angrily refused to see a doctor, saying there was nothing wrong with her.

Debbie found a job stocking shelves in a department store. She used some of the money she was saving for college to move into an apartment. Debbie just couldn't continue with school. She felt alienated, and many of her fellow students were mean and thoughtless. There were times when Debbie hated herself for the way she was feeling, and she often asked herself "Why Me?" She saw her friends having a good time, getting ready for graduation, and making plans for college. Is it going to be like this for the rest of my life? She knew the feelings were not right, but she did not know what to do. If she went to a doctor, he would say she was crazy. And, what could he do about it anyway? Debbie felt so lonely, with no one to turn to.

There was one group of people who did accept Debbie, at least it seemed so on the surface. They also had problems and were shunned by much of society. A person could talk to them and they seemed to have more empathy and understanding. This new group used drugs extensively, and was essentially the school dropouts, the people who did not fit in and who were looked down upon by the majority of other people. They thought Debbie was cool and much of her behavior was similar to behavior exhibited by someone who was high. In fact, Debbie fit right in much of the time. No one made fun of her, and they laughed with her rather than at her.

Initially, Debbie hung out with the group because it was easier to be around other people who were as sick as she was. She started smoking cigarettes because every one else did. Soon, she was smoking two packs a day. She refused the drugs that were offered and put up with the gentle teasing about being straight. The drugs seemed to be constantly abundant and were always offered free. One day Debbie was offered a puff off of a marijuana cigarette and accepted. She took several more puffs and found that she liked the feeling. Within a few days Debbie was a regular marijuana smoker. She discovered that the voices seemed to be less severe when she was high. Her head was more clear and she felt better when she smoked marijuana. It seemed to make her more calm and less tense.

Soon, Debbie was buying marijuana by the bag and smoking several joints a day. It was kind of nice, hanging out with her friends, and getting high all the time. Gradually, Debbie started experimenting with the hard drugs and spending more money. Her friends told her the hard drugs would give her an even greater high and make her forget her troubles. What Debbie did not realize was that, within this group that accepted her, was a small group of individuals who take advantage of others, the people who sell drugs for a living, who use others and discard them when they are no longer useful to them.

It took only a few months for Debbie to go through her entire savings account. Now, she was one of the group that shared her drugs with the new group members. Most of her savings and her salary went to drugs. One evening, after work, Debbie wanted a hit real bad. She was completely out of money and she would not get paid for another week. Tony, her primary drug contact, whom she considered a friend, suggested another way to get drugs.

Tony was more than a simple drug pusher. He was twenty five years old, and had been on his own since he was fifteen. His alcoholic father had kicked him out of the house when he tried to keep his mother from getting beaten by his father. Having had no previous experience on the streets, Tony learned how to survive the hard way. He had been taken advantage of by nearly every street jockey in the city. Tony was smart, and each time someone took advantage of him, he learned something about survival and it never happened twice. He had been beaten up, ended up in the hospital after taking bad drugs, and experienced every possible sexual abuse. Gradually, Tony became one of the most respected street jockeys in the city. He had learned from the best and no one was ever going to take advantage of him again.

There were numerous groups like the one Debbie had joined throughout the city. Tony would go from group to group, passing out free drugs to the newer people, and selling drugs to the ones who were hooked. He had stopped using the hard drugs several years ago because he realized he could not operate effectively if he was addicted. Marijuana was his drug of choice and he continued to smoke it regularly, but carefully.

Drugs was just one of Tony's financial endeavors. He also functioned as a pimp for girls and boys. Tony was bisexual and had worked for a pimp for a few months when he was first starting out. Unlike other pimps, Tony did not keep a stable, and did not try to control the lives of those who worked for him. He would take the money from the johns, call people until he found the right one, and get the two together. He would take twenty five percent of the money. Tony had an excellent reputation among his regular johns and his boys and girls. He never cheated anyone. Tony was also respected for the way he treated people. If a john ever hurt or beat up one of his people, Tony would never deal with him again. It did not make a difference to Tony whether or not the john was a senator or the chief of police. No one hurts his people. The same rule applied to his boys and girls. If any of his people took advantage of a john in any way, Tony would never call him or her again.

Debbie was different from most of the kids with whom Tony came into contact. She never complained about her home and seemed to have enough money for the drugs. It was obvious to everyone that she was crazy, but she seemed to be harmless. She had a great body and Tony knew she could be a real money tree if she worked for him. The johns loved the girls who were young and naive. There was something attractive about having sex with a person who was not experienced. Tony did not think Debbie's being crazy would have a negative impact on her attractiveness to johns. They would just think she was high on something. When Debbie first joined the group Tony had hit on her, as he did with all new kids. The earlier the better. Debbie turned him down and Tony did not make an issue of it. He knew it would only be a matter of time before she ran out of money and came to him, begging for a hit. It had happened many times before and he had learned to be patient. Debbie was different, and Tony knew that when the time came, he had to play it smart and slow, waiting for her to make each step, without pressuring her. She would be worth it.

It seemed easy enough. All Debbie had to do was have sex with Tony and she could have a hit. Debbie was completely out of money. Her parents had told her they would not loan her any more money until she agreed to see a doctor, and there was no way she was going to do that. She knew she would end up in some kind of treatment center if she agreed to see a doctor. Debbie did not know what to do. She wanted a hit so bad, yet she had vowed to herself that she would not have sex until she got married. Just as Tony said, everyone's doing it, and it was no big deal. Debbie looked around the room. All the kids were high, some were making out, and she knew some were having sex in the bedrooms. Tony had a special room where he took people and all the kids talked about how neat it was.

The need for a hit and the atmosphere won, and Debbie reluctantly agreed to have sex with Tony. They walked into his special room and she understood what the other kids were talking about. It was plush, and there was a huge bed in the middle of the room, with mirrors on the ceiling and the walls. Tony had hooked another one. This was probably the biggest high Tony got, when he knew he had brought another person under his spell. It was better than sex or drugs! It was power!!

Tony was very experienced and knew how important the first time was. He offered Debbie any drug she wanted and watched her as she looked over the wide assortment of drugs on the table. It reminded him of a child picking out candy. When she was finished with the hit and seemed to be into her high, Tony asked Debbie to join him in the hot tub. Tony was very gentle with Debbie and they made love for hours, in the tub and on the bed. He also made sure she had as many hits as she wanted. He wanted to make this experience one she would never forget, and wanted to make sure she came back for more. Tony was surprised Debbie was a virgin. It also increased her worth in his mind. His johns would pay big money for her!

After the first time, it was easy to do it again, and Debbie found she enjoyed having sex with Tony. They would have sex several times a day and she had access to all the drugs she wanted. She even thought she was falling in love with him. Tony seemed to accept her as she was, crazy behavior and all. A few weeks later, Tony convinced Debbie to move in with him. She lost her job, and she was now completely dependent on him. Debbie would do anything for Tony, he was so good to her and gave her everything she wanted.

Debbie was stoned all the time now and seemed to live in a dream world. When she was on drugs she seemed to be less anxious, and the voices were less intrusive. She still responded to the voices and was now starting to see spider like things on the wall and floor.

One month after she moved in with Tony, he asked her to do a special favor for him. He said he had this friend who had not had sex since his wife died. The friend was looking for someone special to have sex with him, and Tony wondered if Debbie would help him out. Debbie thought she owed Tony a lot and she felt sorry for his friend. She agreed to have sex with Tony's friend just this one time.

For this first time, Tony had picked one of the johns who he knew would be nice to Debbie, and who would pay double the usual fee if he thought he was getting a virgin. Of course, Tony would keep all the money, since Debbie did not know he was charging for it. She thought she was doing everyone a favor. The john was nice to Debbie and seemed to be very appreciative of her gift. Tony rewarded her with a beautiful bracelet. The next week it was a friend who had trouble getting an erection, and soon Debbie was turning tricks for Tony on a regular basis. As long as Tony provided the drugs and called her his girl, Debbie would do anything to make him happy.

Tony stopped sleeping with Debbie when she became more withdrawn and unresponsive. He always had to ride her about taking care of herself, and even that was becoming more difficult. He rented Debbie an apartment close to his house, and maintained her drug habit as long as she continued to satisfy his customers. Tony took care of her, paid her bills, bought her groceries, and hired someone to clean the apartment. It wasn't long before Debbie's customers started to complain about her smelling bad and being unresponsive in bed. Fewer and fewer customers asked for Debbie and Tony finally decided to dump her. Debbie begged Tony not to put her on the street and take away her drugs. She said she would do anything for him, if he would continue to supply her with drugs. Tony said he needed to cut his losses and that he would take her back if she got her act straightened out.

Debbie tried living on the streets. She offered her body to anybody that came along, but she smelled and looked so bad that she had few takers. She tried living in alleys, inside cardboard boxes, and survived by going through the garbage of restaurants. Most of the street people left her alone because she acted so crazy. With no drugs available, Debbie had to go through withdrawal alone, with no one to help her and no medication to take the pain away. At the age of eighteen, Debbie had hit bottom, and had no idea what to do.

Joan and David were completely shocked when Debbie appeared at their door. She was skinny and pale. Her hair looked like she had not touched it for weeks. Her clothes were filthy and she didn't have any shoes. Debbie had disappeared after she moved out of her apartment and the Simpsons had been looking for her for months. They had been giving her money for several months prior to her moving out, and suspected that the money was being used to maintain her drug habit. The Simpsons got an appointment with a drug counselor recommended by their doctor. He told them to encourage her to seek treatment and, if she refused, to stop giving her money. Sometimes, he said, tough love was the only thing that worked. The Simpsons felt guilty about stopping the money, but they did not know what else they could do. When they tried to talk to Debbie, she would get extremely upset and accuse them of trying to run her life. They really felt guilty when Debbie had moved out of the apartment and they could not locate her. They could envision all kinds of things happening to her, including death. They had called the police, but the police officer they talked to said there was nothing they could do if Debbie was over the age of sixteen and no crime had been committed. The Simpsons had even driven through the worst part of the city, showing Debbie's picture and asking if anyone had seen her.

After presenting herself at the door, Debbie started crying and fell into the arms of Joan, giving up completely. Joan removed Debbie's clothes and got her to take a hot shower. She helped her shampoo her hair and brushed it, just like she did when Debbie was a child. David fixed some hot chocolate and they all three sat down and talked. Debbie told them about the voices, the job, the apartment, and the drugs. She did not tell them about Tony, or about selling herself, or living on the streets. She just said she had been living with some friends. Her parents told her she did the right thing to come home and that they would help her to get treatment.

Now that the voices were with her all the time, Debbie had a hard time resisting them when they would tell her to harm herself. The spiders were still there also. She would often get up off her chair, and act like she was stepping on something, or push something away with her hand. Without drugs to calm her, Debbie felt anxious and tense all the time.

Mental illness had not crossed the minds of Joan and David. They were sure it was drugs. Soon after Debbie moved out of the house, she started associating with the drug users. They agreed, she needed chemical dependency treatment.

Debbie's parents were relieved when she agreed to move back into their home. Now they could help her straighten out her life. She looked so thin, wore strange clothes, and did not seem to care about her appearance. Worst of all, Debbie was a chain smoker. She seemed to have a cigarette in her mouth all the time. She was very offended when the Simpsons asked her to restrict her smoking to her room. Her parents were determined to get Debbie into treatment. This was the day her high school class was graduating. She could still get her GED and go to college if she put her mind to it, Joan thought.

Debbie finally agreed to see the family doctor, Dr. Henderson. Debbie knew something was wrong. She felt terrible, was sleeping all the time, and was not motivated to do anything. She could not believe how low she had sunk, to sell her body and beg on the streets. The positive thing about not being able to obtain drugs was that she had detoxed herself. If anyone had been willing to give her drugs, she would still be hooked and on the streets, selling herself. She looked and smelled so bad that not even the street scum wanted anything to do with her.

Debbie had mixed feelings about Tony. Sure, he had used her, but in a way, she had used him. She remembered the good times of constant sex and drugs. She also remembered the bad times, of getting kicked out of Tony's house, of being sold to other men, of begging on the streets and eating out of garbage cans.

After examining Debbie, Dr. Henderson said, "I can't find anything wrong with Debbie physically. She seems tired and rundown, but nothing more. I'm going to prescribe some vitamins, and I have made an appointment with Dr. Williams. He is a psychiatrist who has an office in this building, and I think he will be able to help you."

It was a month before they could meet with Dr. Williams. In the mean time, Debbie's health improved, thanks to regular meals, vitamins, and the care supplied by her parents. Her psychological state remained the same. Debbie did not seem to be interested in anything, was not concerned about how she looked, and seemed to exist in a world of her own. She continued to have auditory and visual hallucinations, was constantly talking to imaginary people, and seemed to see spiders everywhere. Debbie also became preoccupied with religion, talking about demons, space stations, and getting messages from God. Her parents were sure she was still using drugs. Debbie's smoking was very disturbing to her parents. No one else in the house smoked and the house reeked of stale smoke. Reluctantly, her parents bought Debbie cigarettes. They felt very guilty about loosing track of her for two months, and they were not about to go through that again.

Dr. Williams examined Debbie and later met with her and her parents. "Debbie," said Dr. Williams, "it is a little early to give a definitive diagnosis, but your symptoms suggest that you have a mental illness called schizophrenia. We usually wait until a person has exhibited the symptoms for six months before we give such a diagnosis, but your symptoms are so characteristic of the illness that I feel confident in giving you this information. And, you did say that you started hearing voices over six months ago."

Debbie and her parents could not believe what they were hearing. Mental illness had never entered their minds until now. They had gone along with the appointment with Dr. Williams because their family doctor had suggested it, and they trusted him. Drugs they could possibly understand, but not mental illness.

"Well," said Debbie, "There is no way that I am mentally ill." "But, let's say I am, how did I get it?" "I know it is hard to accept," Dr. Williams responded. "No one wants to believe they are mentally ill. It isn't like a virus, you don't get it from someone else. There is still a lot we don't know, but there is strong evidence that it starts with hereditary predisposition to schizophrenia. Sometimes the illness begins after some type of emotional trauma or tension.

"Are there medications that don't have side effects?" asked Debbie, feeling very fearful about having to take the medications. "None of the current medications are without side effects," responded Dr. Williams, "but there will be newer medications coming out in the future which may not have as many side effects."

"I'm willing to try anything to get rid of these voices," said Debbie, "but I'm afraid of what the medications might do to me." "We try to take every precaution," responded Dr. Williams. "We will start you out on a small dose and gradually build up to what we call a therapeutic amount where the drug should be working. We will watch for side effects and we will take blood samples to see how much of the drug you have in your system. We will also prescribe another medication which should take care of most of the side effects. If you work closely with us Debbie, I think you will find the medication to be very useful."

Debbie was given a prescription and was told not to mix the medication with alcohol or street drugs. On the way home Joan said she did not know of anyone in her family who had a history of mental illness. David said his paternal grandmother died when he was six years old and he could remember relatives talking about her bizarre behavior.

Chapter Four

Susan's Story

"I can't take it anymore!" Susan told Dr. Williams. "I just don't have the energy it takes to make life work. I'm a bad parent and a bad woman! My son would be better off if he had a different mother."

This was Susan's third admission for a suicide attempt. She had taken all of the depression medication that was left in the bottle, along with a pint of vodka. Her best friend, Diane, found Susan unconscious on her bed with the empty pill bottle next to her. Susan's two year old son was sleeping in the crib. Diane called 911 and Susan was taken to the emergency room. Her stomach was pumped, she was given activated charcoal to neutralize the remaining medication, and she was admitted to the intensive care unit. Dr. Williams was called after Susan requested to see him.

Susan was sitting on the edge of her bed, her head in her hands, staring at the floor. Dr. Williams pulled a chair up next to her. She must have lost twenty pounds since the last time I saw her, he said to himself. "You've lost more weight," he said. " I'm just not hungry" She said. "We are going to have to monitor your food intake and weight, just like we did the last time you were here" said Dr. Williams. "Whatever," Susan said, in a very soft voice. Her responses are very flat, showing no affect. She avoids eye contact and her face is expressionless when she takes her hands away. She looks like someone who has completely given up, and who doesn't care what happens to herself.

"Who is taking care of the baby?" asks Dr. Williams. "Diane is. She is such a good friend and we have so much in common." Susan said. "You two have been good friends for a long time," said Dr. Williams. "Yea, ever since we met at the halfway house when we were kids. Social Services tried to break us up, but we wouldn't let them. Diane is really the only good thing that has ever happened to me, except for my baby. We are always helping each other out."

"Are you still drinking?" asked Dr. Williams. "Yea, sometimes it's the only thing that will take the pain away. Alcohol and drugs make me numb, and for me, that's a good feeling." "Are you still having flashbacks?" asked Dr. Williams. "Of the rape?" "Yea, I can still hear, see, and smell the bastard. I don't think that will ever go away. I even have nightmares about him coming back and raping me again. I think that's why I always have to have a man with me, even if most of them are jerks."

"Did you go back to your boyfriend after you left the hospital last time?" Asked Dr. Williams. "Of course, he is the father of my baby," responded Susan. "Even after he beat you? continued Dr. Williams.

Susan looked at Dr. Williams and smiled a little. "After you left that day, Ben showed up at my hospital room with a big bouquet of roses and a box of my favorite chocolates. He was crying, apologized for hitting me, and begged me to come back. He looked like a little boy. I felt so sorry for him." "But he has beaten you several times. Twice you ended up in the emergency room." Dr. Williams said, trying to understand something that has always avoided his comprehension. "You are a nice guy for trying to help me, Dr. Williams, but you just don't get it. It isn't always Ben's fault. I do some really stupid things and I don't blame Ben for getting mad. Besides, my dad always hit my mom." "That doesn't make it right." Said Dr. Williams. "Has Ben hit your son?" continued Dr. Williams. Susan hesitated, "Now let me get this straight, what I tell you is strictly confidential, but, if I so much as mention child abuse, you have to report it, right?" "Yes" said Dr. Williams. "Then Ben has never hit our baby." said Susan. "That gives me my answer, but I guess I can't report what did not happen." said Dr. Williams. "But," he continued, "if I ever see a suspicious bruise on your baby, I will report it." "I know you don't believe me, but the abuse will only get worse until Ben gets treatment or goes to jail." "You don't have to worry about Ben anymore, he's out of my life," Susan said.

"Well, let's get on with the interview." said Dr. Williams. "The last time we met, we talked about changing some of your habits in order to avoid relapsing. Were you able to find different kinds of recreation, or different friends?" "Diane is really the only friend I have." said Susan. "And, I really like going down to the Club, one of the local bars. It's really the only fun I have. It's the only good thing I remember about my childhood. I remember mom and dad taking me to Mac's bar. Everyone called my name and said hello, like they do to Norm on Cheers. People would give me money and candy. It was like a second home to me. Every time Johnny Cash would sing that song, A Boy Named Sue, everybody would sing along, point to me, and laugh."

"Is it hard to control your drinking when everyone else around you is drinking?" asked Dr. Williams. "Yea, sometimes I start to feel sorry for myself, and ask my self, WHY ME?; Why do I have to be depressed? Why do I have to be alcoholic? Why do I have to take these damn meds all the time? And, then I tell myself one drink won't hurt. But, I would not know what to do even if I wanted to quit the bar scene. Where would I spend my time? I know what you are saying, that I need to change my lifestyle, but it is very hard to change my friends and my habits."

"Tell me what happened when you left the hospital the last time." Dr. Williams asked. "Let's see, that was last April, if I remember correctly," responded Susan. "Ben picked me up and we returned to the apartment. He was really nice to me for a few months, except he was more controlling. He tried to keep me from seeing Diane and told me he knew what was best for me. Whenever he wanted to control me, he reminded me that I am mentally ill, and he would tell me I can't take care of myself or my baby. I know he meant well, and wanted to help, but it was very irritating. No one knows what is best for another person. Things started to go wrong after Ben lost his job. He blamed me for everything, and he started to get more physical. Every time we had an argument, it would end up with some type of abuse, verbal or physical. Many times he would threaten me with violence if I did not shut up. Ben insisted on having sex when he felt like it, and the way he liked to do it, and he never asked me what I liked. He even started to use force in our sexual relationship, in a playful way. I finally got tired of his constant anger and hostility and asked the court for a restraining order. I really loved Ben, but we just couldn't live together." What Susan did not tell Dr. Williams was that Ben started to abuse their baby. It got to the point that she was afraid to leave the two alone together. She knew that Dr. Williams would report Ben to the police if she told him the truth, and she did not want Ben to get into any more trouble. Susan was also worried that Ben might try to hurt her or her baby if she told Dr. Williams the truth.

"Did the restraining order work?" asked Dr. Williams, "They never worked before with Ben." "I know, I asked myself the same question," responded Susan. "I was worried for several days after I got the restraining order. In the past, Ben has broken the door down, or caught me outside the grocery store on the corner and beaten me. I finally figured it out, with a little help. After I got the restraining order, Diane said she saw Ben at the bar down the street. He was real cozy with a bleached blond. Diane said he was really putting on a show for her because he knew she would tell me. His hands were all over this blond, and she was not objecting. In a way, it was a relief to know that Ben had found someone else to abuse. To be honest though, I did feel a little jealous. We had lived together, on and off, for three years, and he was the father of my child."

"I haven't seen Ben for six months," continued Susan, "so I guess it's all over." "Does he help you with the baby?" asked Dr Williams. "You mean child support? That's a laugh! He can't even take care of himself. Every time he gets a job he either quits or gets fired. Ben has been living off other people since he quit high school. As you know, he is very good looking, and he has a great body. He has no problem finding a woman who will let him live with her. I'm surprised we stayed together as long as we did. He usually lives with a woman for a few months, and then moves on to another one. It's hard to explain, but Ben has this way about him that makes him very attractive to women. I sure fell for him! "

"So, what have you been doing for the last six months?" asked Dr. Williams. "Well," responded Susan, smiling a little, "I think I found a new guy. I'm not sure, but it looks promising." "Where did you meet him," asked Dr. Williams. "At the Club," Susan said, looking sheepishly. "I know you don't want me to hang around the Club, but it's the only place I have fun. I know everybody there, and I feel secure at the Club. I have really tried to find some other place to hang out. I went to a young adult group at the local church. I attended several meetings of two different singles clubs. I feel so weird there. I feel like I stick out, and that everyone is looking at me and wondering what I am doing there. Most of those people have never been through anything close to what I have experienced. It's hard to talk to people about something when they can't understand it. It seemed like, every time I told someone about myself, they would back off and find something else to do or someone else to talk to. Not once did someone invite me to have coffee with them or to see them outside of the meeting. People like to go to places where they feel accepted, and I feel accepted at the Club. There are people there who have been through a lot more than me. My problems are nothing compared to some people! "

"Speaking of problems, how did you end up here this time?" asked Dr. Williams. "I went off my meds again," responded Susan. "I know, you have repeatedly told me that I will probably have to take my meds for the rest of my life. I had been feeling good for several weeks, and I decided to stop taking the meds to see if it would make any difference. It did not make any difference for several days, so I thought I didn't need them. After a week or two, I slowly started to feel worse. I found myself becoming more irritable with my son, yelling at him, spanking him more. I couldn't concentrate or even make minor decisions. I was tired all the time, and couldn't eat. I seemed to have backaches and headaches all the time. Time seemed to pass so slow, and the world seemed so dreary and meaningless. I lost all interest in life and couldn't feel any pleasure in anything, even my son. Diane was a jewel, as usual. She would stop in every day, change the baby's diapers and feed him. Then she would fix me something to eat. She tried to get me to make an appointment with you, but I was too embarrassed to let you see me in this condition, after all our discussions about medication."

You should never feel embarrassed about talking to me," Dr. Williams said. "I am very accustomed to people going off their medication. That is probably the primary reason people return to the hospital. Usually, it is because people don't like the side effects of the medication they are on, but it is not unusual for people to think they don't need the medication any longer. Some people will experiment with their medications, trying to find the lowest possible dosage that will work for them. And, there are always the people who don't think they are mentally ill, and who throw their medication away as soon as they leave the hospital."

Dr. Williams looked at Susan's arms. "I don't see any fresh cuts. When is the last time you cut?" "You know, I wondered about that myself," responded Susan. "I haven't cut since I left Ben. He used to get terribly angry at me when I cut. He couldn't stand to see me bleed. He would have to leave the room. How could my cutting be related to Ben?" "Maybe you don't get anxious now that you don't have to worry about him hitting you," Dr. Williams said. "That's possible," said Susan. " It is hard to figure out. Sometimes I can go for months without cutting. Other times, I seem to have to cut every few days. I'm going to have to be more careful, now that my son is getting older. I don't want him to see me cut."

"So, what plans do you have for the future," asked Dr. Williams. "Now that I'm going to live, I suppose I have to develop some plans, Are you going to insist I go to a halfway house, or can I go back to my apartment and my son?," Susan asked in a pleading manner. "It will take a few weeks to stabilize you on your medication. Lets see how well you do in the hospital. I won't eliminate your returning to your apartment as an alternative, but I will need some assurances that you will be able to take care of yourself. If you go home, you may have to go to day treatment and have someone check in on you on a regular basis, at least for the first few months. We also have to be concerned about your son, and your ability to take care of him. What would have happened if Diane did not come by? You would have been dead and your son's health and life would have been in jeopardy. When a person gets as depressed as you did, they can not think straight."

"Do I have to go to groups while I'm here? Can't I just talk to you?" Susan asked. "I hate to sit in groups and talk about my problems." "Medication is just one part of our treatment program," responded Dr. Williams. "You need to learn to recognize the early signs of depression so you can take some action before the illness immobilizes you. Your recent suicide attempt is evidence that you are unable to intervene when your symptoms start to occur. You could also use help in learning how to cope with your anger and shame. You have obvious errors in your thinking, jumping to discouraging conclusions. You seem to notice mainly the most unpleasant aspects of a situation, and then make pessimistic generalizations. If you try to work with the system, you will find you will become less isolated and self preoccupied. The group can be a mutual support system, if you let it. It helps you see that others have similar problems and that you are not alone. The group process often stirs up feelings that provide insight into past and present relationships." "Ok, Ok, I'll go to group," Susan said.

Three weeks have passed and Susan is stabilized on her medication. "Can I leave now?" asks Susan. "I think you are ready," responds Dr. Williams. "How do you feel?" "I'm not depressed any more. I am looking forward to getting out and moving back to my apartment. Diane brought my son to see me almost every day this past week. I want to leave as soon as possible so I can start taking care of my son again. I miss him so much!.." "Is that your new boyfriend I saw you with the other day?" asked Dr. Williams. "Yes, isn't he good looking? He came to see me several times while I was here. His name is Andy and I think I am in love with him. We are talking about living together when I get out." "Isn't that kind of fast? Didn't you just meet him a few months ago?" asked Dr. Williams. "I knew you would say that," responded Susan. "How did you meet him?" Asked Dr. Williams. "We met at the Club. He was drinking then, but he recently completed chemical dependency treatment and he goes to Alcoholics Anonymous three times a week. He hasn't taken a drink in six weeks. We can help each other because we are both chemically dependent and we know how important it is not to take that first drink. We understand each other, and we have similar problems. Isn't that important in a relationship?" "Yes," said Dr. Williams, "but there are lots of things that are necessary to make a relationship work. I think you should take it slow with Andy and get to know him well before you start to live together. You haven't had a good history in picking men. You told me that the last time you were in the hospital." "But Andy's different," Susan said. Dr. Williams shook his head, he had heard the same words many times before, and he was very familiar with the results. These women usually picked the same kind of men and almost always ended up in an abusive, alcoholic relationship. It was a mystery to him why they picked the same kind of men until he asked a patient one time. She said he was the only person who would want to be with her. Her self concept was so low that she thought this was the only person who would accept her.

"What do you know about Andy?" asked Dr. Williams. "He has been married once and has two children, a boy five and a girl who is seven. His wife has custody of the children, but he has visiting privileges. When we start living together, he wants to be able to bring his children to our house for weekends. It will be good for my son, to have other children to play with. He is temporarily unemployed, but he has applied for several jobs and hopes to get one soon. He works in construction and his last job was as a taper with a dry wall company. He likes to work on cars and to race them." "Has he ever hit his ex-wife?" asked Dr. Williams. "He said they have had a few fights, but she always started it." "Has he ever hit his ex-wife?" Dr. Williams asked again. "Yes," Susan said, reluctantly, "but that doesn't mean he will hit me. He said he has learned his lesson, and that it only happened when he was drinking."

"Do I have to go to day treatment?" asked Susan. "Yes, at least for a few months, until we are sure you are back on your feet. It will only be three times a week, for a few hours each day." "But I can't stand being around all those crazy people," Susan said. "I thought you liked to be around people with similar problems," said Dr. Williams. "I might have mental problems, but I'm not crazy like most of them in day treatment." Susan said. "Well, it will only be for a little while and you should try to make the best of it, rather than fight it." Dr. Williams said. "I'm also going to have a public health nurse stop by your house every day to make sure you are taking your medication, and to see how you and your son are doing. The social worker will give you the date and time for your first outpatient appointment with me, as well as your first day treatment appointment. We will send you home with a weeks worth of medication, and a prescription for a month of medication. You can't overdose on the medication I put you on, but you can get sick if you drink alcohol while you are taking this medication, so be careful."

"Thanks, Dr. Williams, see you in a month."

Chapter Five

Jason's Story

Jason's mother and Aunt Emily are sitting in the living room having coffee. "Thanks for flying up here so quickly. I was not sure you would come after the way we treated you. I just don't know what to do about Jason. He is a different person than the Jason we raised and loved. It's not that we don't love him, he just makes it so hard to do so."

I know" said Emily, "As soon as you called I knew exactly what had happened." "It took me many years to finally accept my mental illness. It is one of the hardest things to do, to come to the realization that you are mentally ill and different from everyone else. Most people don't understand the illness and people avoid you like you have the plague when they find out. There is nothing you can do about it, you are stuck with it for life. It is a life long disease that can be controlled, but not cured. When you are off your medication you really believe all the things you tell other people. For example, I really believe that I am the Virgin Mary when I'm sick. I really believe that I can control other people and read their thoughts!"

"Do you mean that Jason really believes that he can be a professional quarterback, that he can run a business in his present condition?" asked Sally. "Those delusions, and that's what the professionals call them, aren't really that bad compared to the ones I have heard." "How about 'king of the universe', or 'receiving messages through your teeth', or 'thinking the FBI is after you,' or 'believing you are in a television and the only way out is to break the screen.'" "You won't believe some of the things I did" responded Emily. "I tried to start numerous businesses when I was manic, always falling flat on my face. I have a reputation throughout Florida. No one will loan me money or give me credit. It is probably best this way. Now I can't get into any more trouble. The most terrifying thing for me is what the professionals call racing thoughts. The thoughts go so fast that you can't remember a thought you had two words ago. You get so confused that you want to commit suicide just to get away from the feeling." "Did you try to commit suicide?" asked Sally. "Yes" responded Emily, "several times." "I'm too afraid to use a gun or knife. I usually overdose on whatever I can find in the medicine cabinet. I can't seem to go all the way. I call 911 right before I pass out. The problem with trying to commit suicide is that it gives the doctor an excuse to commit me to a mental hospital. The peaks and valleys are unbelievable. One moment you can be on top of the world, the next moment you want to end it all."

"Oh I feel so bad," said Sally. "We knew something was wrong with you but we just ignored it and went on with our lives. We were angry with you because we thought you could control your behavior and you were acting that way because you were selfish and did not care about anyone else. And, as it ends up, we were the selfish ones!" "Don't feel bad," replied Emily, "There really was not much you could have done if you had tried. I was in complete denial at the time and I doubt if anyone could have helped me. Look how many hospitalizations it has taken for me to get this far."

"Do you think it will take Jason that long? I'm sorry, there I go acting selfish again. This change in him has just turned our family upside down. All our energy is directed at trying to help him and worrying about what he will do next. Sonja and Tammy complain that Jason is all we think and talk about. It used to be sports and now it is his strange behavior."

"I would like to talk to him some time," Emily said. " I don't know if I can help him or not, but I would like to try. It is different now. People know a lot more about mental illness and they are developing new medications every year. If he is like I was, it may take him several years to get through the denial and start to accept the illness and the fact that it will be with him the rest of his life. Like most of us, Jason probably goes off his medication at the first opportunity. It usually takes several weeks for the mental illness to return because the medication stays in the body for awhile."

"How about relationships? It must be hard on the people you are close to. Jason has destroyed the one good relationship he had." Sally enquired. "Talk about disasters, I have destroyed every one of my relationships!" responded Emily. "I had some good men too. Believe it or not, I can be very attractive to men. I met my first guy in a library of all places. I went to college several times. I never got a degree but I have enough credits for a Ph.D. Anyway, he was a real hunk! We lived together for six months and talked about getting married. One night I decide to stop off at the local bar for a drink. I meet another man, we talk, I suggest we fly to San Francisco and we stay there for a week. I return home and try to explain what happened to my college man and he walks out. When I am manic I am very unpredictable and usually aggressive, always wanting to pick a fight. I guess that is true of most manics." "Its certainly true of Jason," responded Sally.

"What does Jason think about his medication?" asked Emily. "He hates them," Sally replied. "He begs the doctor to reduce them when he is in the hospital and quits taking them as soon as he can. He says they make him feel funny." "That's exactly the way I was," said Emily. "I don't know why it takes us so long to finally realize we need the meds. I have met a lot of young people in the hospitals and it seems like every one of them has gone through the denial and rejecting the medication. When I first got sick they gave me some medications that made me feel awful. I hated the side effects. Then lithium came along

and wasn't so bad. I have been on my medication for two years now."
"Every mentally ill person is faced with the same quandary when they get out of the hospital, to take the medication and put up with the side effects, or to quit the medication and be crazy. Believe me, it is not an easy decision. The need to be normal is powerful. Remember when you were a child and you hated to be different? You start to feel good and you quit the meds, thinking you don't need them any more. If you are manic like Jason and I, you miss that powerful euphoria you feel when you are manic. You feel like you can do anything, be anybody, and you have tremendous energy. The meds take that feeling away and you live a very boring life compared to being manic. Some very important people in history have been diagnosed with the bipolar illness, including some politicians and several artists."

"I really think the future is bright for Jason," continued Emily. "They are coming out with new medications all the time, and the new meds have fewer side effects. New discoveries are pouring out of neuroscience labs, and new technology is allowing researchers to understand the precise mechanisms that occur in the brain. I just hope it doesn't take Jason as long to cooperate with the doctors as it did me." "That's what I'm worried about," said Sally. "It's so hard to get him to cooperate. He gets so angry when we try to help him! Several times I thought he and his father or his uncle would get into a fight. After talking to you I have a better understanding of what he is going through, but it will still be hard to be around him when he is manic. It's like he is trying to antagonize us. He has a cigarette in his mouth all the time, looks terrible with his long hair, and his clothes look like he got them at the Goodwill store. His language is filthy and his sisters can't stand to be around him. They used to worship him when he was in high school. Now they are embarrassed to tell anyone he is their brother. "

"That's one reason I stayed away," said Emily. "I knew mom and dad would not want to have anything to do with me. I didn't want to face rejection and criticism from any of you. I remember how close we were at one time. I guess we will never have that again." "I want to try to get it back," replied Sally. "If you can forgive us for the way we treated you. I want to be a complete family again."

Chapter Six

Debbie's Story

"I'm queen of the universe and no one can tell me what to do," Debbie said, sitting next to Ralph, her drinking buddy. They were sitting in the alley, passing a bottle of wine back and forth. They had just finished eating a grand dinner of sirloin steak, mashed potatoes, green beans, and french bread. The restaurant must have had a special on sirloin steak because the garbage can was full of partially eaten steaks. "If anyone messes with me I'll call my special forces in and kill every last one of them." Debbie continued. Ralph shook his head in agreement and said, "I'll protect you Deb, I won't let those bastards take you in." There was a big difference between Ralph and Debbie. Ralph was drunk and would say anything to pacify Debbie, knowing all along that it was just the alcohol talking. Debbie was drunk too, but she really believed everything she was saying. They met on the streets several years ago and became close friends and drinking buddies. Ralph had tried to touch her breast one time, but gave up after she slapped his hand. They were also neighbors, having cardboard boxes next to each other down by the tracks.

Ralph saw himself as Debbie's protector. In fact, he had gotten himself beaten up several times trying to protect her. Sure she was crazy, but she always treated him with respect. Ralph was twenty years older than Debbie and he had been an alcoholic all of his adult life. His parents were alcoholic, as were three of his four siblings. Jennifer, his oldest sister, was the only one in the family who wasn't addicted to something. Ralph received $450 a month in social security payments and has been doing so for ten years because he is an alcoholic. He tried working several times but could not seem to hold a job. Either he quit because he did not like the work or he was fired for not coming to work, or coming to work drunk. Ralph was close to setting the record for detox admissions. He had been taken to or admitted himself to the detoxification center seventy eight times. The county had given up trying to treat his alcoholism. He had been referred to chemical dependency treatment six times. On four of those occasions he left treatment before it was completed. He was craving for a drink so bad that he could not stand it, and just walked away. The two times he did complete treatment he was in a locked unit and was not able to leave treatment when he wanted a drink. After completing treatment the second time he was able to stay sober and hold a job for six months, the longest time he had been sober since he was seventeen. One day, after his boss yelled at him, Ralph told him to shove the job and went straight to a bar.

Ralph tried living in several sober houses, where the only requirement was no drinking, but that never lasted very long. Ralph preferred living on the streets. He did not have to pay for housing and could use all his social security money for booze and essentials. Ralph also tried living in the shelter provided by the city, but he found the shelter was more dangerous than the streets. He had been robbed twice in the shelter. In the streets you could pick who you were going to associate with and sleep next to. Ralph and several of his friends had selected a spot near the tracks which was isolated and protected from the weather. The police seldom bothered them, especially if they were quiet and stayed to themselves. The only problem was that the high school bullies found them. The kids seemed to get a big thrill out of beating up bums. While Ralph and Debbie were eating outside of the restaurant one day, five of the local bullies found their sleeping quarters, burned all their belongings, and sent three of Ralph's friends to the hospital.

Debbie liked Ralph because he never asked for anything, except for that one time he touched her breast. He accepted her the way she was and never suggested that she get help or take her medication. She hated the medication and quit taking it as soon as possible after each hospitalization. Whenever she saw her parents, which wasn't very often now, all they could talk about was how important it was for her to take her medication. "My parents should get a shot of Haldol just to see what it feels like," Debbie told Ralph. "They have never experienced feeling like a zombie, walking with a shuffle, getting terrible cramps in the head and neck, feeling restless and pacing all the time."

What Debbie hated the worst was being committed. "When you are committed, and the judge says you have to take medication, you lose all control over what people can do to you." Debbie often complained to Ralph about her treatment by the courts because he would always listen to her and support her. The law says a person has to be a danger to herself or others in order to be committed, but Debbie thought they had stretched the law the two times she had been committed. The first time, her parents convinced the court to commit her because she wasn't taking care of herself and she was putting her life in danger by living on the streets. She was very angry at her parents, screamed at them, and told them she would never see them again if they ever tried to commit her again. She had to take "those damn medications" for six months and she hated every minute of it. If a person did not take the medications orally they would be given a shot that lasted two weeks. Debbie hated needles and she fought with staff every time they tried to give her a shot. When it was time for her to get a shot, they would call for extra staff because they knew it would be a battle. Hospital staff would grab her by the arms and legs and put her face down on the bed. They would pull her pants down and give her a shot with five or six people holding her down. Debbie finally agreed to take the medication orally when she realized she couldn't win.

The second time Debbie was committed the police found her rummaging through the garbage. When they asked her what she was doing she threatened to get a gun and "blow the fucker's heads off." The police were not certain who she was talking about and decided to take her to the crisis unit. Debbie told the psychiatrist she feared for her life because she was queen of the universe and that there was an international plot to kill her and take over the world. She stated she would kill herself if her enemies tortured her too much. She reported that her enemies had killed her parents and siblings and that she was the only family member left. Debbie said she took food from the garbage cans because regular food was poisoned. She refused to take medications because they "mess up my thinking" and "I don't feel right on them."

After experiencing several hospitalizations, and having to take medication each time, Debbie decided the best way to avoid hospitals was to be a street person. By not associating with normal people Debbie thought she had a better chance of remaining free. And, she kind of liked this lifestyle, if she could avoid the people who tried to take advantage of her. Being a female on the streets was not easy. It seemed like every male she met tried to get into her pants until she learned how to turn them off. Debbie's unkempt look was not entirely unintentional. She quickly discovered that the worse she looked and smelled the more she was left alone.

Debbie was not able to completely avoid trouble. After her first hospitalization Debbie returned to the home of her parents. She did not hear voices and she did not see strange things like spiders as long as she took her medication, but she still stayed by herself a lot, was emotionally unresponsive, and smoked all the time. After a few weeks, Debbie got tired of her parents hovering over her, making sure she took her medication, and trying to get her to cut down on her smoking. One day she packed a duffle bag and left home while her parents were working, leaving her medication on the dresser in her room. Her parents became very concerned when they returned home and realized Debbie had left. They called the police, but they said there was nothing they could do since Debbie was an adult and there was no crime committed. Her parents spent several days and nights looking for her, but they could find no trace of her.

The first night Debbie was on her own she met James. He saw her walking down the street and asked her if she wanted a ride. She declined so he stopped the car and offered to take her to dinner. Debbie was hungry and decided that having dinner with a stranger was not too dangerous, especially with a lot of other people around. As soon as James spotted Debbie he decided to pursue her for his stable of women. He had done this many times before and knew exactly what to say and do. Debbie was good looking, young, and the duffle bag she carried was a dead give away. She was running away from something, and needed help. He would be her knight in shining armor.

Debbie and James stayed in the restaurant two hours. For the entire time, James' primary goal was to gain her confidence. It would be several weeks before the medication Debbie had been taking would stop working completely, so she appeared to be fairly normal. The more James talked to Debbie the more strange she appeared, but it wasn't her head he was interested in. James asked Debbie if she had a place to stay and suggested a local motel when she told him she had no plans. He offered to give her a ride to the motel and she reluctantly agreed. On the way to the motel James said he had to stop at his apartment. He pulled into a quiet street, got out of the car, and locked the doors with her inside. He went into a building and returned with two men. James asked Debbie if she wanted to go up to his apartment. When she declined, they grabbed her and carried her into the building, with one man holding his hand over her mouth so she would not scream.

The men carried Debbie into an apartment, took her into a bedroom, and locked the door. An hour later, James walked into the bedroom, took his clothes off and raped her. He was followed by the other two men. Over the next week, Debbie was locked in the bedroom, and was repeatedly sexually assaulted by numerous men. It was James' intention to condition Debbie to every possible sexual act he could think of so she would feel comfortable with any request made by her future johns when he turned her out.

There was one thing James failed to consider. The longer Debbie was held in the room, the more bizarre her behavior became, and the more she smelled and refused to take care of herself. Several times James beat Debbie in an effort to get her to take care of herself, but nothing seemed to work, not even being nice to her. James' friends refused to have sex with her, even though it was free. James had never experienced this before and had a hard time giving up on considerable potential income. After a few weeks, Debbie was completely psychotic, hearing voices, seeing spiders all over the room, and talking about being queen of the universe. It became obvious to James that he had better cut his losses. He gave her back her clothes and duffle bag, and told one of his friends to drop her off down by the tracks. That's where she met Ralph.

Ralph saw Debbie wandering around and asked her to share some of his food. She screamed and ran away from him. He told her he would place some food on a rock and walked several yards away. Debbie grabbed the food and ran. For several days they went through this ritual of Ralph leaving food on the rock and Debbie eating it only after he walked a safe distance away. It took several weeks for Ralph to gain Debbie's confidence to the point where they both ate off the same rock at the same time. Over the next several months Ralph taught Debbie all the nuances of being a street person, how to get food, where to sleep, and most importantly, how to be safe.

Chapter Seven

Mennon Hospital

Mennon Hospital   June 3, 1994
Admission Information
Jason Henderson #25136

This twenty nine year old male was committed from Watson county as mentally ill and chemically dependent. He was initially hospitalized at West Rockford Hospital. He was brought to West Rockford by police after smashing his pickup into the rear end of a car on purpose. According to the police report, Jason became very angry with the driver of the other vehicle when he pulled in front of Jason's pickup. Jason proceeded to try to hit the car with his truck several times, causing considerable damage to both vehicles. When the two vehicles stopped, Jason got out of his truck and walked over to the other vehicle, screaming at the driver and telling him to get out of the car and fight. The other driver was scared and locked the car doors. Jason proceeded to kick the car and broke the headlights. When the police arrived, Jason started yelling at them, telling them to stay away from him, that he was a karate expert, and that he would hurt them if they came near him. Reinforcements were called in. Jason was well known to the police and when they told him they were going to take him to the hospital he started to run away. It took several police to subdue Jason and he hit one policeman in the right temple as they were trying to get him under control. Jason fought with the policemen for several minutes until they were finally able to handcuff him.

At West Rockford Hospital Jason was manic, with delusions of grandeur, and was very intrusive. He bragged about all the money he had and all the businesses he owned. He said he was going to call his lawyer and sue the police and the hospital. Jason was aggressive at the hospital, threatened staff, and refused to cooperate with the admission process. He refused to take the medications which were offered and exposed himself to female clients and staff. It was necessary to seclude Jason in order to protect him and the other clients.

Mrs. Henderson, Jason's mother, reported that he had been off his medication for several months. His parents went to see him the day before he was hospitalized and found him to be very manic, saying things that did not make sense, and behaving in a very hostile manner. She said they knew at that time that it would only be a matter of time before he got into trouble. Mrs. Henderson stated that Jason had been living in subsidized apartments, giving him reduced rent. He has held several jobs, but none of them for very long. He either quit or was fired. She went on to say that they have had to learn the hard way that the only way they can get Jason into a hospital is for him to do something wrong. She said it was a miracle that Jason or someone else has not been killed. She said it would be easier on everyone if this type of behavior could be avoided by taking the preventive approach and hospitalizing people as soon as they go off their medications.

According to Mrs. Henderson, Jason responds well to medication. He had a three year period of not being hospitalized because he cooperated with taking his medication. His parents are very concerned about him because he seems to be worse every time he gets hospitalized. She said it seems to take longer each time to get him stabilized.

Beginning in 1984, Jason has been hospitalized a total of ten times at West Rockford Hospital. His diagnosis has consistently been Bipolar Disorder, Manic. Jason has a history of abusing chemicals, primarily alcohol and marijuana, and has been treated for chemical dependency on two occasions, leaving both times before treatment was completed. Jason was also hospitalized at Mennon Hospital in 1989 and 1992, and in Chicago, Los Angeles, and Denver. Each time he was hospitalized out of state, his father flew out and brought him back.

Jason reintegrates fairly quickly when he is stabilized on his medication. His manic behavior is beginning to subside already, although he continues to talk about being pursued by several professional sports teams. He is currently taking a combination of medications, a combination which has been successful in previous hospitalizations. Jason is also starting to complain about the side effects of the medications and requesting a reduction in the amount of medication which is prescribed.

Mark Breem
Social Worker

Mennon Hospital   June 5, 1994
Admission Information
Susan Kreeger #216394

This twenty nine year old mother of two was committed from West Rockford Hospital in Watson County for the third time. While living at a halfway house, Susan walked to the local drugstore and purchased three packages of over-the-counter sleeping pills. She returned to her room in the halfway house and took all the sleeping pills, along with a pint of vodka she had hidden in her room. Halfway house staff, noticing that Susan's speech was slurred, questioned her. Susan admitted taking the sleeping pills. 911 was called and Susan was transported to the emergency ward at West Rockford Hospital. She was unable to ambulate and was incontinent of urine. Her stomach was pumped and she was admitted to the intensive care unit. Later, after she was stabilized, Susan was transferred to the Mental Health unit at West Rockford.

Susan has a long history of depression dating back to early childhood. She was removed from her home at the age of six because her parents were unable to take care of her. Her mother was depressed and alcoholic and her father was alcoholic and physically abusive to Susan's mother. Susan was raised in a series of foster homes and halfway houses. She has numerous scars on both arms and on the inside of both of her legs from cuts she made with sharp objects. She claims the cutting temporarily relieves feelings of anxiety and tension, especially when she can't get hold of alcohol to medicate her feelings.

Susan states she was raped at the age of twelve by the son of her foster parents, but the authorities took no action. The person who abused her was later found guilty of sexually abusing several other girls in the neighborhood.

Susan attempted suicide on ten occasions. She tried to hang herself two times when she was previously hospitalized at Mennon Hospital. On one occasion she tied the cord of her pajamas around the closet pole. She was discovered by her room mate standing on a chair, with the cord around her neck, getting ready to push the chair away. On the other occasion, she tied her shoe laces together, tied one end to the door knob, threw the shoe strings over the door, and tied them around her neck, planning on sitting down and hanging herself. She was found by a staff member, while making rounds of the sleeping rooms, right after she had finished tying the string around her neck. Susan cut her wrists when she was 19 years old and tried to asphyxiate herself with a plastic bag when she was 22 years old. On six other occasions, Susan tried to overdose on prescription or over the counter medication, usually accompanied by alcohol.

Each time Susan attempted suicide she was hospitalized. She has also been hospitalized for major depression on five occasions. When she is depressed, Susan has a hard time getting out of bed. She can not concentrate, has very low motivation and energy, and tends to isolate herself.

Susan has never been married, but has been involved in several abusive relationships. She has two children by two different men. The children are boys, ages 5 and 7, and are currently living in foster homes. The children have lived with their mother on an intermittent basis, between hospitalizations. She currently has visiting privileges and hopes to regain custody when she is released from the hospital. Susan admits to using alcohol to medicate her depression and anxiety, but denies she is chemically dependent. She has never been treated for chemical abuse.

Susan has been treated with ECT the last two times she was hospitalized at Mennon. She appears to be the most successful after treatment with ECT and states that she prefers shock treatments over medication. Twelve weekly ECT treatments, followed by monthly maintenance treatments has proven to be effective.

Mark Breem
Social Worker

Mennon Hospital   June 9, 1994
Admission Information
Deborah Simpson #21195

This is the fourth commitment for this twenty nine year old female resident of Watson County. She was transferred from West Rockford Hospital where she had been hospitalized since May 13, 1997. The police were called to investigate an apparent homeless woman looking for food in garbage cans. She was extremely dirty and had a very foul odor about her. When the police tried to put Debbie in the car, she started swearing at the deputies and swinging wildly. She stated she was queen of the world and that they had better leave her alone or she would call her army.

When Debbie was admitted to West Rockford Hospital, her clothing was filthy and she appeared to have urinated in her clothing. She refused a medical examination and would not take medical tests. She laughed for no apparent reason and constantly moved her hands as if she was swatting flies in the air. Debbie stated that she liked her lifestyle and could see nothing wrong with finding food in garbage cans. She stated she had been living this way for years and that it did not bother anyone. When staff tried to get her clothes off and give her a bath, she kicked a nurse in the face and it was necessary to take her to seclusion in restraints. Emergency medication was ordered, and Debbie was transferred to Mennon Hospital.

After two weeks on medication, Debbie became more cooperative and signed a release of information so staff could communicate with her parents. According to Mr. and Mrs. Simpson, Debbie has been mentally ill since she was about 17 years old. Dr. Williams, at West Rockford Hospital, had diagnosed Debbie as schizophrenic when she was 18 years old. She had a child when she was 21 years old and placed the child for adoption. She can no longer have children after deciding to have a tubal ligation five years ago.

Debbie has been hospitalized at three other state hospitals for periods of 3-8 months. She has been hospitalized at West Rockford Hospital on eleven occasions, and at Ferndale Hospital six times. Debbie has also lived in five different halfway houses after her hospitalizations. She is extremely difficult to work with in the community, preferring to associate with the derelicts who live near the tracks. Debbie has run away from every community facility in which she has been placed. She is currently taking a combination of medications. Debbie has a history of responding to neuroleptic medication without any major side effects, but she states she hates the medication and can't stand the side effects. She says she would prefer to be crazy rather than take "that damn stuff". Debbie is usually cooperative in the institution, once she is stabilized on her medication. She stops her medication the first chance she gets when she returns to the community. We will try one of the new medications to see if she has a better response and less side effects.

Mark Breem
Social Worker

"I sure would like to get into her pants!" Jason said, as he watched a new patient walk by. "You want to get into everyone's pants," said Debbie, sipping her coffee. "Are you trying to set a record?" she asked Jason. "What's wrong with wanting to fuck?" responded Jason. "It's a normal human function. Where would mankind be if it weren't for fucking?" Debbie shook her head as she smiled at Susan. The three of them were having coffee in the patient lounge at Mennon Hospital. All three of them had recently been admitted to the hospital and were going through the evaluation phase, prior to being discharged back to the community or transferred to a treatment unit in the hospital.

"What were you trying to prove the other day?" asked Debbie to Jason. "What do you mean?" asked Jason, knowing full well what she was talking about. "When all those staff put you in seclusion," said Debbie. "The fuckers would not leave me alone. I told them not to touch me. They would not let me keep my knife. It's just a little pocket knife I use to clean my fingernails. They said it could be used as a weapon. What the fuck! Can you see me trying to fight someone with a little pocket knife? If I'm going to fight someone it will be with my hands or feet. Did you know that I have a black belt in Karate?" Not another one, Susan thought to herself, I wonder how many guys have told me they were black belts. "Eric bugs the hell out of me," continued Jason. "He thinks he is such a big shit. I would like to catch him outside. I would beat the hell out of him." "I think he is pretty nice," said Susan.

"He is one of the best staff members on the admission unit." "Bullshit," responded Jason. "He just treats you nice because you are a female. Every time I come in here he gets in my face." "You aren't exactly a model patient when you come in here," responded Susan.

"Did you see what I did to the security room on admissions?" asked Jason proudly. "I really tore that hole apart. They had to move me to three different security rooms before I got tired of tearing them up. There isn't a security room in the state that I haven't destroyed. I know how to beat this system. Let me tell you how to get out of these places. When you first come in you act as wild as you can. Then, when you are your normal self, they think they have helped you, and they let you go." "If you are so smart," said Debbie, "Why do you keep coming back?"

"Oh shit," said Jason, "Here comes Tony." Tony was almost a permanent fixture at the hospital. He had been in and out of mental hospitals for thirty years and none of the medications seemed to work very well with him. He had been discharged to the community many times, and always came back a few weeks after he was discharged. He would act out and cause trouble just enough to get sent back. Tony repeatedly told staff that he liked it at the hospital and didn't want to leave. Because of the emphasis on getting patients back to the community as soon as possible, and using the least restrictive level of treatment, the staff were obligated to keep trying to place Tony in the community.

Tony had a terrible habit that bothered a lot of staff and patients. He was continually asking other people for money or cigarettes. When patients are on county assistance, as Tony was, they are given $55 dollars a month to spend on anything they want. Tony was unable to budget his money and usually had the money spent the first week, leaving three more weeks to beg before he received his allowance again. All day, every day, Tony went from person to person begging for money or cigarettes. When no one would give him a cigarette, he would look through ash trays, trying to find a cigarette butt that still had a few puffs left on it.

"Get the fuck away from me," Jason yelled in a threatening manner. Tony quickly backed off and approached another patient at the next table, getting a similar response. "I hate it when he does that," said Jason. "It seems like everyone here is constantly asking for something." "Let him alone," said Debbie, "That's just the way he is." "Yeah," said Susan, "Some of us don't have parents to give us money like you do. There are a lot of us who are completely dependent on the county allowance. Figure it out. A pack of cigarettes cost two-fifty. Take two-fifty times thirty days ant that's more than we get from the county. And, a lot of us smoke more than one pack a day."

"I know how you can get a free pack," said Jason, with a smirk on his face. "How," asked Susan. "Lets go behind the powerhouse and I'll show you," responded Jason. "Jesus Christ," exclaimed Debbie, "Is that all you think about?" "What else is there?" answered Jason.

Debbie, Jason, and Susan had known each other, or at least known about each other, since elementary school. They were not aware that they were all born at the same hospital, on the same day, at approximately the same time. Their paths had crossed enough, through previous hospitalizations, that they were familiar with each other enough to be considered friends. Having recently arrived at the hospital, their psychiatric symptoms were still very evident. Jason was very aggressive and hypersexual, Debbie was still seeing and hearing things that are not real, and Susan was still depressed.

"I'm out of smokes, can I borrow one?" Jason asks. Susan hands him one, smiling. "After that tirade you just went through with Tony, you're asking for a cigarette? exclaimed Debbie. "Fuck you," responded Jason, Susan knows I'll pay her back." "I expect to get some money any time now." Jason had called his parents the previous night, asking them to send him more money. He spent his last ten dollars on a pizza party several patients organized the previous evening. "I hate to ask my mom for anything," said Jason. "She always makes a big deal about how I waste money. She almost had a heart attack when I told her I sold the coat she gave me for Christmas." "What did you sell it for?" asked Susan. "A bag of marijuana," responded Jason. Susan rolls her eyes, "No wonder she was mad." "She doesn't know what I sold it for, but I really needed to get high! I would have sold two coats for a bag!"

"What are we having for dinner tonight?" asks Debbie. "I think it is tater tot hot dish," responded Susan. "I hope it's better than that crap we had last night," said Jason. "It tasted like SOS." "What's that?" asks Susan. "Shit on a shingle," responds Jason. "I liked it," Debbie said. "It was better than a lot of things I've eaten." "I don't know how you can go through garbage and hang around bums all the time," Susan said. "I could never do that." "It's not so bad once you get used to it," said Debbie. "Restaurants throw a lot of good food away. Several times I found steaks that were hardly touched. It sure beats the food at the shelter. Besides, the shelter is one of most dangerous places in the city, especially if you are a woman. Every time I go there someone hits on me. I've screwed lots of guys just to keep from getting beat up, and some of them hit me anyway. As for the "bums" as you call them, some of my best friends live near the tracks. They treat me with respect and not one has ever tried to harm me. They accept me as I am and don't try to change me. It's the times I get away from the tracks that I have all the problems. My parents, the police, the doctors, the social workers, they all want to change me."

Jason looked at Debbie but did not say anything. He thought to himself, "Who would want to fuck her. She is so messed up. She is always talking to herself, doesn't take care of herself, wears terrible stinking clothes. She used to be pretty. She has sure gone down hill since high school."

Debbie had been on psychiatric medications for two weeks, since she first entered West Rockford Hospital, prior to being transferred to Mennon Hospital. The voices she heard, the spiders she saw, the delusions about being queen of the world, all positive symptoms of schizophrenia, were beginning to decrease. She still had some of the negative symptoms of schizophrenia, which are less responsive to medication. Debbie had trouble concentrating, and seldom combed her hair or brushed her teeth. She still had to be reminded to take a bath and to wash her clothes.

Debbie's parents had finally accepted her mental illness and tried to relate to her on her terms. They still loved her, and tried to help her when she asked for help. Every time her parents offered help Debbie seemed to get more angry and their relationship got worse. Seeing her this way was very painful but Debbie's parents did not know what else to do. In order to protect themselves emotionally, they had to distance themselves from her. It hurt too much to see their daughter as a homeless person who ate out of trash cans and who put herself in such dangerous situations. As a street person, they knew she was in constant danger and it would not have surprised them to see her name in the paper as having died from a mugging or freezing to death.

On numerous occasions, Debbie's parents had found her in the streets and tried to get her to come home with them or go to a hospital. She would get extremely angry at them, calling them terrible names, and making statements that did not make sense, such as being queen of the world and had an army that would protect her. Debbie's parents would send her money when she requested it, but they had given up hope that she would change.

Debbie was angry at Susan for bringing up the garbage cans. Now she wished she had not told anyone about how she survived on the streets. In a way, she was proud of her survival methods and her ability to survive without depending on anyone. "Talk about me!" Debbie said, "I'm not sure your life has been any better," looking at Susan. "You jump from one asshole to another, expecting them to take care of you. And what happens? They beat the shit out of you! You let men walk all over you."

It's true, thought Susan, I've been kicked around my whole life. This last time was the worst, she said to herself. She had been living with Jim for six months, hoping to establish some stability so she could get her children out of foster care. One night, she didn't cook the meat enough and he proceeded to beat her so bad that she was in the hospital for a week. Of course, he brought flowers and said he was sorry, blaming his hitting her on drugs. She had heard that before, many times. It's the drugs, or the alcohol, or some other excuse. Her abusers always seemed to be in denial. They just could not accept the fact that they had a problem. Jim even pimped her one night. He got her high on crack and passed her around to his friends, charging them twenty dollars for a fuck. The following day Susan was shocked and embarrassed about what she had done. She could not believe how low she had slipped in her life.

"Why do I pick these guys?" Susan asked herself. She had asked herself that same question many times before, and she thought she knew the reason. Susan had recently met with Mr. Breen, the social worker, and told him she did not deserve any better. "What nice guy would want to be with me? I'm a looser, she said to herself. I'm always depressed. I have these cuts all over my body. I've got two kids that I can't take care of properly. I'm always trying to commit suicide and I can't even do that right. The person that said life sucks was sure right."

Susan was not sure what she was going to do about Jim. She knew he was still drinking and using drugs. She wanted to go back to him, but realistically she knew that nothing had changed. If she went back to him, he would beat her up again. It was the same with all the men she had lived with and all the men she had known, including her father. Jim was still living in their apartment and all of her clothes and furniture were still there. He called her several times, asking for forgiveness and wanting to get back together. She was beginning to soften up again and was thinking about going back to him one more time. Maybe it really was the drugs that caused him to behave that way. He can be nice when he wants to. Besides, she could not ask the county for any help. Susan was afraid to contact the county because it might prejudice them against returning her children to her. "The less the county knows the better!"

"I wish I could get rid of these flashbacks" said Susan. "What flashbacks" asked Jason. "From when I was raped at the age of twelve." Susan told Jason and Debbie about her rape. "It has been almost twenty years since it happened and I feel like it just happened yesterday. I was so scared of that boy and no one did anything about it. His mom called me a whore and kicked me out of the foster home. The social worker just moved me to another foster home." "What are the flashbacks like?" asked Debbie. "I get scared, real frightened," responded Susan. "My heart starts beating fast and I want to run away. I feel panicky, and think about killing myself to get away from all the pain."

"What are all those cuts from?" asked Jason. Susan was wearing a short sleeve blouse. The scars ran up and down the inside of both arms. Susan was embarrassed about the scars and usually wore long sleeves to hide them. It was a warm day and she had decided to wear short sleeves. Now she regretted her decision. "These are from cutting myself. I started cutting when I was about twelve years old. They aren't suicide attempts, except for these two." Susan points to two cuts on her wrists. "Why do you do that?" Asked Jason. "I don't know for sure," responds Susan. "It just makes me feel good for awhile. When I get real anxious and upset, like when I have flashbacks, the cutting seems to release the tension, at least for awhile. It's like the tension flows out with the blood. As I watch the blood ooze out, I can almost feel my body relax. I know it sounds weird, but that's why I cut myself." "But," continued Susan, feeling a little proud, "I have not cut myself for a year. I didn't even cut myself when I was living with Jim, and I was constantly afraid of getting beat up."

"That's certainly a reason to feel upset," Debbie said. "Are you going to back to him?" "I don't want to, but all my clothes and things are in the apartment. If he thought for a moment that I was not coming back he would throw everything out in the street." "What a nice guy!" Debbie said sarcastically. "Somehow, I have to get him to leave me without beating me up. Alcohol and drugs are more important to him than I am. He said he is thinking about moving back to Chicago. Maybe he will move before I get out. Then I would not have to worry so much." "What an asshole," replied Debbie.

"Yesterday in group Mr. Brown said something interesting," said Susan. "What was that?" asked Jason. "Well, it went something like this. We were talking about family issues and abuse and he said he was always amazed how we hurt the people we love the most. That's certainly true for me. The people who have hurt me the most are the people I have been closest to, beginning with my parents. Look at how people treat their children and their loved ones. It's almost like a love-hate relationship," Susan said. "As I look back on my relationship with my parents," Debbie said, "I can't remember when they ever really hurt me. They have always tried to help me. It's me who has hurt them, over and over again. I have called them every name in the book and treated them like shit, and they still stuck by me. More than anything, I resented their trying to help." "Me too," said Jason, "My parents may have misunderstood me, but they have been there when I needed them. Sometimes I can't believe the hell I have put them through."

"What's wrong with that guy?" asked Jason, watching another patient walk into the coffee shop. "He has what they call tardive dyskinesia," said Debbie. It's a side effect of the medication he was put on years ago. That's one reason I hate to take the shit, the side effects make me feel terrible and I don't want to look like him." "How did you get so smart?" asked Jason. "I know a lot about mental illness," responded Debbie. "Every time I go into a hospital, I try to read all I can about it, and if I don't know something I ask the staff. I consider myself a student of mental illness. I'll bet I can tell you what is wrong with most people in the hospital," said Debbie. "If you are so smart, how come you keep coming back?" asked Jason. "Like I said, I can't stand the side effects," replied Debbie.

Henry, the patient with tardive dyskinesia, walked over to the food counter and stood in line. His tongue went in and out of his mouth. He smacked his lips, and his face grimaced as if he was in pain. Every so often Henry's head would go back and he would thrust his hips out, shaking and flinging his hands in the air. "He's really a nice guy," said Susan. "Before he became mentally ill he was an elementary school teacher. He says he wants to go back to teaching someday but I don"t see how he can." "Yeah," replied Debbie, "tardive dyskinesia is usually permanent. "How often does that happen?" asked Jason. "A lot of people get it from neuroleptic medication, but it usually isn't that bad and it can usually be controlled by other medication," replied Debbie.

"And I thought akathesia and dry mouth were bad," said Jason. "I can't seem to sit still. It feels like my skin is crawling or like little electrical currents are running through my body. As soon as I sit down, my legs start moving up and down. I complained to Dr. Hansen, and he said to give the medication time to work." "That's what he tells everyone," said Debbie. "Dr. Hanson gave me some medication to counteract the akathesia, but I told him to change the meds or I would spit them out," continued Jason. "I hope I never look like Henry, that's really scary."

"It's really a hard decision," said Debbie, "to take the medication and put up with the side effects or to be mentally ill. I usually choose to be mentally ill. I'm more comfortable in my illness, and at the time, I don't know the difference. I think I'm normal and everyone else is strange." They all laugh.

"Dr. Hansen did say that he is thinking about putting me on a new medication that just came out." Debbie said. "It's supposed to help me with all my symptoms and the side effects are not as bad as some of the older meds. The only side effects are insomnia and feeling tired all the time, and even those don't happen with everyone who takes the medication. Who knows, I might even try to stay on my meds when I leave, if they can find one that won't make me feel so miserable."

"I'm not on anything right now," said Susan. "They are going to start shock treatments next week and they want me off all meds before they start." "How can you take those things?" asked Jason. "I don't want my body attached to a bunch of wires. Does anyone ever get electrocuted?" "It's not as bad as it sounds," said Susan. "For me it works better than medication and there are no side effects, except for some loss of memory after each treatment. What happens is that they pass an electric current through my brain several times a week for three weeks. The electric current apparently causes a seizure which somehow takes away the depression. Then I take maintenance treatments every two weeks, and then monthly to keep my depression from coming back. The last time I took shock treatments my depression did not return for six months." "From what I have been reading," chimed in Debbie, "electro shock treatments are coming back again. In many cases they work better than meds."

"I don't think I could ever let someone do that to me," said Jason. "The idea of shock treatments is almost as old as bleeding people to help them. It's archaic." "But it works for me," countered Susan.

"So what girl are you after this week?" asked Debbie, secretly wishing it were her. Jason was good looking and had a great body. He lifted weights almost every day. "A new girl just came in," responded Jason. "She is a little young for me, but she looks fantastic. I think she is here for depression and suicide attempts, something about breaking up with her boyfriend. She has guys hanging around her all the time, and I need to make my move soon, before she finds someone else."

Jason was starting to accept the fact that he was mentally ill and that he was never going to be a professional athlete. He knew he was a different person on medication, but his life seemed so dull without the manic feeling. He liked to feel on top of the world, to stay up all night, to chase women. To think he could do anything he wanted to was exhilarating. Jason was also aware that his old friends wanted nothing to do with him when he was manic. He is very scary when he is aggressive and his temper flares up easily when he does not get his way. When he is manic, Jason has a bad habit of coming on to every woman he meets, including the wives and girlfriends of his friends, often resulting in arguments and bad feelings. Most of his friends from high school are married, have children, and are working. Although his high school exploits carried him a long way, Jason had developed a different reputation. He is now known as a womanizer and an obnoxious bully. Most of his old friends stopped hanging around with him, and the people that did associate with him were known as loosers in the community. Jason's present lifestyle consisted of hanging around bars, getting into fights, and picking up women for one night stands.

Jason was like two different people, a Dr. Jekyll and Mr. Hyde. When he was stabilized on his medication, he was nice and pleasant, courteous to others, and respectful. When he was in his manic stage, which was most of the time, he was unlikable, foul mouthed, nasty, and intimidating. What friends he had left were afraid to approach him because they did not know which Jason would respond. Jason had an inkling that other people saw him this way, yet he was so much into his manic behavior that he ignored the feelings of others and would ride roughshod over anyone that got into his way. This is a primary characteristic of mental illness, whether it be bipolar, schizophrenia , or depression. The emotions and the manner of thinking that accompany the illness are so strong and definite, that the individual who is experiencing the illness is not aware of anything else at the time. The illness is so all encompassing that there is no room for another way of behaving or thinking.

In many ways, Jason envied his old friends. He often asked himself why he couldn't be married and have children. Why Me? he asked himself, but only when he was stabilized and not manic. Jason seldom talked about the pain he felt when others rejected him. He wanted so badly to be like everyone else, and it was hard to accept that he would never fit in. Even his family seemed to have less interest in him and he seldom saw his favorite uncle Ray anymore. The next generation of children were starting to get involved in sports now and his father and Ray were spending a lot of time with them, just like they did when Jason was that age. It seemed like the world was passing him by and he was stuck in one place, with no way out. For three years he stayed on his meds, held down a job, and tried to be normal. It was very hard to do, taking medication every day, knowing that other people were walking on eggshells when they were around him, never knowing how he would behave.

Jason had embarrassed his parents so often that they were embarrassed to be seen is public with him. The last time was one of the worst. Jason had gone to a little league game to watch his nephew play baseball. Jason's father and uncle were coaching the team. Many of his relatives were in the stands, including his mother and his sisters. Jason stopped taking his medication two months before and he was in a very manic condition, feeling aggressive and infallible. His mother could easily tell he was off his medication, but she had learned the hard way not to mention it to him in front of other people. Throughout much of the game, Jason yelled at the umpire, questioning his calls, and calling him names. His mother and sisters tried to get him to be quiet, but he told them to mind their own business. He received numerous dirty looks from his father and uncle. On one particular call, involving Jason's nephew, Jason became so incensed that he walked out on the field and confronted the umpire. His father and uncle ran onto the field just as Jason took a swing at the umpire. They tackled Jason and held him on the ground. Jason was yelling at them, calling them names, and threatening them. The police were called, and took Jason away in handcuffs.

Jason was determined to make it this time. He was getting sick of hospitals and all the petty rules and restrictions. He was beginning to accept the fact that the only way he was going to stay out of hospitals was to take his medication. His aunt Emily told him that ten years ago, but he did not believe her. With all the research that was going on, Jason was hoping for a long lasting medication that had no side effects.

"OK smart ass, you think you are so smart," Jason said to Debbie, smiling. "What's wrong with the guy that just walked in? He looks pretty normal to me." Debbie smiled, knowing exactly what his problem was because she had just talked to him an hour ago. "That's Howard," Debbie responded. "He is obsessive-compulsive. Notice how careful he walks, he never touches a crack in the floor. He will turn around and walk for miles just to keep from touching a crack. He is also worried about picking up germs. He washes his hands all day long and uses paper towels to open doors. If you look at his hands you will notice how red they are from constant washing. I read where it is very hard to cure. For the person who has it, it is all consuming and very self destructive. An obsession is where you think about something in a persistent manner, and compulsion is where a person acts on the obsession. It seems to relieve their anxiety when they keep repeating an act."

"Wow," said Susan, I'm impressed. You really have been reading up on mental illness. I thought you were just bragging, like when you say you are queen of the world." Debbie smiled and continued with her explanation. "Other examples of obsessive-compulsive behavior are eating only a few carefully selected foods, constantly checking to see if things are in their right place, calling someone to see if your thoughts and actions are correct, and plugging and unplugging electrical appliances over and over. The last time I was here, continued Debbie, this guy would not go to the bathroom. He would shit in paper cups and hide the cups in his room. It drove the staff nuts. His room mate didn't care for it either." "Ah come on, you're bullshitting me," said Jason. "No" responded Debbie, "go ask Mr. Breem if you don't believe me."

"What group do you have next?" asked Susan. "Personal Issues," replied Debbie. "I really get sick of the same old thing over and over again. I wish they would come up with something new. I have played those occupational therapy games so often that I bet I could lead the group. It's like all the staff were trained at the same place and they are afraid to try something different. You play the same game, watch the same videos, read the same handouts in every hospital and day treatment program I have ever been in."

"I got something out of the last session on relationships," said Susan. "It was just like they were talking to me. The hard part is using what you learn in the hospital after you leave. How does a person change the way she has been acting her whole life? It's really hard for me," declared Susan. "Yeah" said Debbie, "It took me thirty years to get to this point. How do they expect us to change in three months.?"

"A person doesn't think about changing when he is sick," said Jason. "You think everything is the way it is supposed to be and there is no reason to change. The only time changing the way you act comes to mind is when you are in the hospital, or jail sometimes," Jason said smiling.

"It's time for group," said Susan. "One more smoke," said Jason, "It's OK if we are a few minutes late." "Did you ever try to quit smoking?" asked Susan. "Yeah," said Jason, "One time I quit for two months. It was hell. I was crawling the wall. All I could think about was having a cigarette. It was worse than not drinking." "I quit for six months once," said Susan. "After my first husband broke my jaw I said to hell with it and went back to smoking and drinking. I figured at the rate I was going I was not going to live long anyway, so why worry about my health. I'm so sick of men. Sometimes I wish I was a lesbian, then I wouldn't need a man." "They beat each other up too," said Debbie. "Yeah," but not as much as men," countered Susan. "I've seen a lot of lesbians have great relationships with no violence. They respect each other and have fun together." "Have you seen Jonell on the phone lately?" asked Jason. "Every time she talks to her lesbian lover she starts crying. It's not all roses on that side either."

"Gay guys are nice to," said Debbie. "When I was in my early twenties, I was trying to find Mr. Right. It seemed like every nice guy turned out to be gay. It was the assholes who were straight." "Hey now," responded Jason, "I'm straight and see what a nice guy I am!" "See what I mean?," said Debbie, smiling, "Case closed."

"What are you guys doing tonight?" asked Debbie. "There is a sign up sheet for going to the movie downtown," said Jason. "I think I'll sign up, but I hate to be seen with the other patients and ride in the bus with the hospital name on it." "Yeah," said Susan, "Everyone stares at us and some of the kids in town make fun of some of the patients. I stopped going downtown on the bus for that reason. I wished we could go by ourselves instead of in such a large group. I guess it's the only way to get everyone off grounds. I think I will wait until my friend comes up and go down town with her."

"There's a dance tomorrow night," said Jason. "Maybe I can dance with the new girl. She is really sharp looking, just my type." Susan smiled and shook her head. Jason had asked her to have sex with him several times before he gave up and went on to ask other patients. She had a hard time saying no, but the last incident with her boyfriend was so fresh in her mind that she did not want to get involved again. And, Jason had a temper that was almost as bad as her boyfriend's. Throughout the years she had seen Jason loose his temper several times, and he could really be mean.

"Did you hear what happened to Dean?" asked Jason. "No what?" responded Susan. "He went wild the other night. He ripped all the pictures off the walls in the hallway and threw a chair through the window. It took six staff to take him down and he was fighting and screaming all the way." "Sounds like you," said Debbie. Jason smiled and continued, "They gave him a shot to calm him down and they had to carry him to the seclusion room on a stretcher. He broke the light in the seclusion room and tried to kick the door down. The staff had to go in, take him down again and transfer him to another security room. He almost beat my record! He is a big guy too. I wouldn't want to tangle with him. The other day he accused me of being a spy for the FBI and said he was going to get me. I slept with the dresser in front of the door that night. He even scares me, the way he stares at me. I hope he gets better fast for my sake!"

"Why don't they take you guys to jail when you do that?" asked Debbie. "I have ended up in jail for a lot less. "They are afraid to keep us in jail," responded Jason. "I learned a long time ago that the way to get out of jail is to act crazy or suicidal. They will quickly move you to a mental health unit. The Jailor doesn't want anything to do with mental illness. The staff have learned that too. They don't even call the cops unless it is very serious."

"Well, we are late for group. Lets get going." said Susan. All three get up and walk out of the coffee shop, returning to the living unit.

Chapter Eight

Discharge

Debbie, Jason, and Susan have been hospitalized for almost two months. They are stabilized and their symptoms are under control. They are in the discharge planning process and are meeting in the coffee shop for the last time prior to being discharged.

"Did you ever make it with that new girl?" asked Debbie. "No," responded Jason. "She wouldn't even have coffee with me. I couldn't believe it. I must be loosing my touch. She said I was too old for her. She wasn't here for very long anyway. She went back to live with her parents and said she was going to return to college next semester. I don't know why she was here in the first place. She seemed to have it all together. But, I am getting along real well with Kim. I have almost got her talked into living with me when we get out." "Why is she here?" asked Susan. "Some kind of eating disorder, combined with alcoholism." "She sure is skinny," said Debbie. "I don't think she weighs 90 pounds." "I've heard her throwing up in the bathroom after she eats," said Susan. "That's supposed to hurt your throat and rot your teeth." "Yeah," said Jason, "but she is really nice and cute."

"Did you know that if two mentally ill people have children, the chances of the children having a mental illness is almost 50 percent?" said Debbie. "Who said anything about having children!" exclaimed Jason. "We just want to live together! Besides, Kim said she was determined to get over her eating problem. She said she was sick and tired of feeling that way and going through treatment." "How many of us have made that statement," said Debbie.

"I noticed you were getting pretty close to Joel." Jason said, looking at Susan. "Not really," replied Susan. "He keeps asking me to be his girlfriend and I am afraid to say no. I worry about hurting his feelings. He seems so fragile. The smallest things seem to get him upset." "Why is he here?" asked Debbie. "I thought you knew everything." said Jason, sarcastically. "That's why I ask questions asshole." responded Debbie. "He said he acted crazy to get out of jail." continued Susan." "When he was in jail he threatened to commit suicide, so they sent him here. He said it worked for him the last time he was in jail too. Now that he has a reputation of being crazy and suicidal, it doesn't take much for him to get out of jail. "

"What did Joel go to jail for?" asked Debbie, looking at Jason, expecting him to make another smart comment. "He pulled a gun on his ex-wife's boyfriend and threatened to kill him, "said Susan. "I guess he has a real temper. He violated a court order to stay away from his ex-wife the first time he was in jail." "Sounds like one of your old boyfriends," said Jason. "Yes, but Joel is nice to me and said his ex-wife was a real bitch." responded Susan. "You aren't falling for that line again are you?" asked Debbie. "That should be a red flag for you. You should run every time you hear that line." "I suppose," said Susan. "That seems to be the kind of guy I attract, and am attracted to. I always think I can change them and that they won't treat me that way. That's the way my father was too, and my mother never learned either."

"Can you believe Sheril?" Jason said. "What do you mean?" asked Susan. "She told me she had fourteen different alters!" "What's an alter?" Susan asked. "It's a personality. She is one of those people who have multiple personalities," Jason replied. "That's no worse than you thinking you are a professional athlete," Debbie said smiling. "Or you thinking you are queen of the universe," replies Jason, taking a mock bow. "What causes a multiple personality?" asked Susan. "According to Sheril, she was sexually abused by her father when she was a child." Debbie said. "I read somewhere that a multiple personality results when a person can't deal with a traumatic experience they had as a child. Some people think it's just a fad. I read an article in the newspaper about two people who said their psychiatrist convinced them they had multiple personalities and that they were abused as children. For some reason, satanic worship is usually involved." "Does Dr. Hanson beleive in it?" asked Susan. "Sheril said he told her she was schizophrenic and that he did not believe in multiple personalities, and I agree with him." replied Debbie. "It looks to me like she can turn the personalities on and off . She said she wants to go to Carlton Center, a treatment center that specializes in multiple personalities. Her doctor in the community told her about the program and she is determined to go there."

"What happened between you and Paul the other night?" Debbie asked Jason. "Oh, he is a real asshole," replied Jason. "He is one of those staff that goes strictly by the rule book. I can't stand him." "At least you know where he is coming from," Susan said. "I would prefer to have him on duty rather than Hank. Hank has his own set of rules and lets most people do anything they want. With Hank, you never know where you stand." "Yeah," replied Jason, but Paul goes overboard. I was one minute late for the smoke porch and Paul would not unlock the door for me. I had to wait another hour before I could smoke. I hate these petty rules. I'll be glad when I get out of here!"

"When are you going to leave?" asked Debbie. "Next Thursday," responded Jason. "I'm going back to my apartment and the discount store has agreed to take me back if I agree to stay on my meds. I was surprised to hear that they would let me work there again after the names I called my supervisor. They said I was a good worker when I take my meds. The meds are working pretty good now, and the side effects are not too bad. I get thirsty a lot and my hand shakes a little. The worst part about staying on medication is that life seems so dull. I like it when I'm high and have a lot of energy. I guess I go too far though, and make every one mad at me. Another thing I have to put up with is having my blood drawn every month to make sure the lithium is at the right level. Too much lithium can cause kidney damage and seizures."

"How are you getting along with your parents," asked Susan. "Pretty good," replied Jason. "I had two weekend passes to their house and they are going to pick me up Thursday and take me to my apartment. Dad was really mad at me after the incident at the ball game. I guess I embarrassed the whole family. That's another reason I have to stay on my meds. I love my parents and they have tried to help me so many times. I don't want to hurt them anymore."

"Didn't your aunt have the same kind of problem," asked Debbie. "Yeah," replied Jason. "After I got sick my aunt told my mom about her history of having a bipolar illness and all the problems and hospitalizations. She has gone through hell too. I guess she was so manic and wild one time that they had to tie her to her bed for days. She responds to meds the way I do. We are OK as long as we take meds, we just don't enjoy life as much. What a choice! Take your meds and live a boring life, or enjoy life and take your chances on coming back here. Some people have the added burden of putting up with all those side effects. That has to be a real tough choice." "Yeah," said Debbie, "You don't know you are sick when you are not taking medication. At the time, the way you are feeling and acting seems to be the way life really is. I can't believe some of the things people told me I have said and done." "You were really strange when you came in," said Jason. "I was?" replied Debbie. "Yeah, a person couldn't even talk to you or understand what you were talking about. It was like you were in your own world," said Jason.

"My illness even resulted in some positive things happening," said Jason. My mom talking to my aunt helped my parents understand and accept my illness, and also brought my aunt back into the family. Now she writes to my mom and visits for the holidays. We have had some nice long talks about our illness, and she has helped me a lot. She is really a great lady. I am even thinking about going to Florida to live with her. She invited me to come down, and said we could help each other when we start to get manic. I don't know though, when I get manic no one can talk to me, probably not even her."

"Aren't you getting out pretty soon?" asked Jason, looking at Debbie. "I'm leaving next week too," responded Debbie. "Can you believe it? My parents are going to let me live with them! We had three good weekend passes together, and they can't get over how good I look. I got all my teeth fixed, got a permanent, and they bought me all new clothes." "You do look great." said Jason. "How about a date?" They all laughed.

"This medication really works," said Debbie. The first few weeks I was on it I was tired and felt like sleeping all the time, but I don't feel tired anymore. In the past, I never stayed on my medication after I was discharged. I hated the feeling of my arms and legs being stiff all the time. People said I walked like a robot. I could never sit still and it felt like my skin was crawling. I just hated the stuff!"

"My parents said I seem more at ease on this medication," continued Debbie. They are impressed with how much I have improved. I just hope the medication is available at my pharmacy. It is a brand new medication and just went on the market four months ago. Of course, it's so new that they probably don't know all the side effects. It will be just my luck to develop a major side effect after I get discharged. Another problem will be getting my psychiatrist at home to keep the prescription going." "Yeah," said Jason. "Every time I get a new shrink, he seems to want to change the medication. Every doctor seems to have his favorite medication." "That happened to me too," said Susan. "I was feeling really good the last time I got out of Lakeview. The doctor changed my meds and the bottom dropped out of my life. Of course, it's never their fault. It's always something we did."

"What do you plan to do after you leave your parents home? Are you going to return to your favorite lifestyle of being a homeless person.?" Jason asked Debbie. "That lifestyle has it's good and bad points," replied Debbie. "I really don't know what I'm going to do in the long run. I am going to take it one day at a time and see how it goes. I haven't lived with my parents in ten years. Maybe we won't get along. I know they don't like my smoking, and I will not be allowed to smoke in their house. I sure as hell am not going to quit smoking! The social worker wants me to go to a day treatment program at the mental health center three half days a week. I might give that a try just to get out of the house. In the past, I never returned to those programs after the first day. I just told the social worker I would go in order to get out of the hospital. The group stuff is really boring, but I usually get along well with the other clients. Several patients from here will be there after they get discharged so it won't be like I don't know anyone. We always go out for coffee afterwards and that is the highlight for me. I also agreed to see a counselor once a week. I don't know what we are going to talk about, but I'll give it a try too. They also have a supportive employment workshop and I might try working a few hours a day. It will all be a new experience for me. In the past, except for the times I was placed in a halfway house, I quit taking my medication as soon as I was discharged, and returned to the streets. My social worker would make these elaborate plans for me and I wouldn't do anything that was on the plan. I would agree to the plan just to get out, and would take off the first chance I had. This time I'm really going to try to make it."

"How about you, Susan? You must be close to getting out too." Jason said, looking at Susan. "I'm waiting for my boyfriend to move out of our apartment," responded Susan. "He told my social worker he was going back to Chicago, but she said he has not left yet. I'm really afraid to go back to my apartment as long as he is there. He's still drinking and it would only be a matter of time before he hits me if I return to living with him. My children's social worker said I could get the kids back if my boyfriend leaves."

"I saw the kids last weekend," said Debbie. "They sure are cute." "Yeah," said Susan, smiling. "They are my reason for staying alive. If I didn't think I could get my kids back I would have been dead a long time ago. I'm also expecting a big check from social security any time now." "Social security?" asked Jason. "There are a lot of people here who get social security for their mental illness disability. I applied about two years ago and it's taken this long for them to approve my application. The good part is that I get paid beginning the date of my application, so I should get a check for about $10,000!" "Wow," said Jason. "Can I get social security?" "Sure," said Susan, "You should apply too. Like me, you have had a long history of mental illness which affects your ability to work." "What do you plan to do with the money?" asked Debbie. "I have seen some people blow the whole thing on drugs." "I've seen that too," replied Susan. "I want to buy a car."

"Are you all through with those shock treatments?" asked Debbie. "I'm through with the regular ones," responded Susan. "I'm now on what they call maintenance treatment. I receive a treatment every month to keep me from becoming depressed again." "Do you think they work?" asked Jason. "They seem to work for me," replied Susan. "And I don't have to take those medications you two have been cussing."

"It's time for group again," said Debbie. "I have my discharge appointment with Dr. Hanson," said Jason. "This will be the last time I see you two," said Debbie. "I'm going on a long pass to my parents house and then I will be discharged if the pass goes well. "I'm going to miss you two," said Susan, hugging both of them, with tears running down her cheeks. "Good luck," said Jason. "I'm going to need all the luck I can get," responded Debbie. "Remember," said Jason. "One day at a time."

.